School Boards
and School Policy

Marilyn Gittell

with

Maurice R. Berube
Boulton H. Demas
Daniel Flavin
Mark Rosentraub
Adele Spier
David Tatge

Published in cooperation with
the Institute for Community Studies,
Queens College, CUNY

The Praeger Special Studies program—
utilizing the most modern and efficient book
production techniques and a selective
worldwide distribution network—makes
available to the academic, government, and
business communities significant, timely
research in U.S. and international economic, social, and political development.

School Boards and School Policy

An Evaluation of Decentralization in New York City

Praeger Publishers   New York   Washington   London

PRAEGER SPECIAL STUDIES IN U.S. ECONOMIC, SOCIAL, AND POLITICAL ISSUES

PRAEGER PUBLISHERS
111 Fourth Avenue, New York, N.Y. 10003, U.S.A.
5, Cromwell Place, London S.W.7, England

Published in the United States of America in 1973
by Praeger Publishers, Inc.

Library of Congress Catalog Card Number: 72-92475

Printed in the United States of America

For the past two years, New York City has been decentralizing its schools. During that time, we at the Institute for Community Studies, Queens College of the City University of New York have been studying that change. Our assumptions are that what happens in New York's schools will have national import not only for school decentralization but for decentralizing any large urban institution.

The decentralized system is by no means an ideal one. The 1970 State Law creating the decentralized system was in some measure punitive. The legislature took a dim view of the 1968 teacher strike and confrontation in the city over community control. This fore-shadowed elected community boards that would have limited powers. Nevertheless, some boards assumed that deep rooted change was needed and proceeded to act accordingly. Our study records that struggle.

The result is this book. We have employed participant observation along with aggregate data to assess the development and impact of school decentralization in New York City. Countless principals, superintendents, and community leaders have been interviewed. We thank them for their time and patience. Also, Frances Gottfried of the Institute offered valuable suggestions; Ben-David Jampel and Morris Green aided in the field observation; Odarkor Lawson of the Institute helped prepare some tables; and Corinne Willing of the Public Education Association provided invaluable criticisms. One last word of thanks must go to the secretaries who prepared the manuscript, Evelyn Cotler, Harriet Jacobson, Rose Spucches, Emily Stasi, and Stella Sussman.

Marilyn Gittell

LIST OF TABLES

School decentralization in New York City has been avidly watched nationally by educators and governmental decision-makers. It has been considered by many observers to be a populist movement, leading educators and an urban public, largely poor, to reform the schools. It has been regarded as a necessary reform, if not a panacea.

The quintessential question has been educational reform, for, if the advocates of school decentralization and community control were motivated by any overriding altruistic impulse, it was to halt the tide of educational failure. To that educational end, school decentralization was but the political means.

School decentralization has had a long history. For three decades, educational reports stressed the need to divide large urban school districts into smaller, more responsive units. These studies emphasized the idea of administrative flexibility in order to respond to educational needs. "The most fundamental crisis in urban education today," wrote Philadelphia Schools Superintendent Mark Shedd in the magazine Educational Leadership in 1967, "is a failure to produce organizations capable of adapting the program of a given school to the needs of a given child. The trick, then is to remake and revitalize through decentralization the quantitatively massive and qualitatively sluggish school systems . . . to create a climate in which beneficial changes can flourish. . . ."

By the 1960s important studies, such as those by the Women's City Club of New York and the Temporary Commission on City Finances, recommended local control and decentralization. Mayor John V. Lindsay in 1967 was able to obtain an educational mandate from the New York State Legislature to decentralize city schools in the name of community participation. The Mayor appointed a blue ribbon committee—the Mayor's Advisory Panel on Decentralization of New York City Schools, headed by Ford Foundation President McGeorge Bundy—to formulate a plan. The committee's report, Reconnection for Learning, commonly known as the Bundy Report, recommended 33 to 65 school districts managed by elected school boards with powers over budget, curriculum, and personnel.

The Bundy Report galvanized the opposition of the professional groups, such as the United Federation of Teachers (UFT) which was fearful of the implications of public accountability and revisions of the intricate civil service system. The controversy reached crisis proportions in the teachers' strikes of 1968 against one of three experimental ventures in local control—Ocean Hill-Brownsville. The

Ocean Hill board caused the involuntary transfer of 19 educators, only to have the UFT claim that due process rights of teachers were violated.

The confrontation at Ocean Hill-Brownsville was more than a parochial matter concerning transfer procedures. It entailed racial and ethnic and political overtones. Most important, it jeopardized the concept of decentralization. The strike adversely affected the fortunes of a strong decentralization bill, based on the Bundy proposals, in the state legislature. The law that emerged—after years of parental protests, many bills, and much politics—was at best a sad compromise.

We have examined policy in our assessment of school decentralization because we believed this type of study is most fruitful. How did the school decentralization law affect the recruitment and selection of board members? How did the legal matrix set the conditions for community boards to function? And, finally, how did these community boards pursue their policies in three key areas—personnel, budget, and curriculum?

One must be cautious in appraising the impact of the community school boards. No one would argue that it is desirable or necessarily meaningful to conduct a study over the short span of two years, but we believe that one can perceive significant trends on the basis of emerging patterns.

An important note must be made concerning the methodology of this book. The conventional academic criteria, which rely so heavily on the quantitative-aggregate data approach, is only useful in certain circumstances. It is not especially valuable in research involving social change and institutional forms in transition. A growing number of social scientists are perceiving that most research tools are designed to measure the status quo. How do we go about examining and evaluating institutions in flux?

There are no final answers. Many social scientists find themselves groping toward a new methodology. Robert S. Weiss and Martin Rein are indicative of this new breed, when they state in their evaluation of a Model Cities program that the "first difficulty was that institutional change seemed difficult to assess." They call for a "non-experimental methodology for evaluation research [which would be] more qualitative, process-oriented. . . ."[1] Alice Rivlin has noted, "Most social action programs have vague and diverse goals, and agreement on how to measure their success is far from complete. Little serious work has been done to develop the objective measures of performance needed to implement this concept of accountability."[2]

Social change requires a methodology that is process oriented and qualitative. That type of methodology would necessarily rely heavily on field observation and interview and on a participant-observer approach that anthropologists have long used with good results. The community school boards (CSB's) created by the State Legislature were the product of ferment, protest, and change and were intended to replace an outdated system. It was only fitting therefore that this study employ a more qualitative methodology to best interpret that attempt. We have not by any means discarded aggregate data; where appropriate we employ the quantitative approach, but we go beyond it.

In gathering the information for this study, the Institute for Community Studies utilized the participant-observer approach extensively. Research assistants were assigned to each of the 31 districts; they attended meetings and interviewed participants over a two-year period. A total of 156 participants—79 board members and 77 community members—agreed to give institute staff about two hours of their time for formal interviews. (See Table 1.) More than 100 other people could not give the institute the necessary time to answer all questions but were helpful in answering several specific queries. To all these people we owe a debt of thanks.

TABLE 1

Data on Participants Interviewed

		Board Members Interviewed					
Number	Average Age	Children in District	Sex M F		Years Living in District	Hours Spent Weekly on CSB Business	Race
79	42.2	1.45	39	40	20.1	23.7	W-46 B-12 PR-20 O-1

		Community Leaders Interviewed					
Number	Average Age	Children in District	Sex M F		Years Living in District	Hours Spent Weekly on CSB Business	Race
77	38.6	1.6	48	29	12.3	17.5	W-36 B-26 PR-15

The participant-observers also attended 90 meetings of the community school boards in the city. At least one meeting of every board was observed. In addition to these meetings, the institute staff attended several meetings of associations, community groups, and community organizations.

Meetings of CSB's Attended	Average Attendance at CSB Meetings
90	184.3

The study is divided into six sections dealing with the various aspects of school decentralization and the community school boards: (1) Political Participation; (2) Policy: Personnel; (3) Policy: Budget; (4) Policy: Educational Program; (5) Community School Board; and (6) Conclusion.

School Boards
and School Policy

Most of those who supported school decentralization and certainly those who opposed it recognized that the creation of local elected school boards in New York City would move school politics out into the open. Supporters generally concluded that under a centralized system the character of school politics was covert and power was concentrated in the hands of school professionals. The opposition defined professionalism in apolitical terms and described any "outside" involvement as "political," characterizing it with negative and undesirable terms. It would be naive indeed to expect that even the minimal changes called for under the decentralization law would not encourage new political forces to become engaged in school activities. In fact that was what was hoped for—the involvement of new participants.

Political scientists have traditionally described political participation simply as voting: if a citizen exercised his right to vote, he was considered a "good citizen" and a participant in the democratic system of government. Refusing to vote, or failure to appear at the polls, has usually carried with it a connotation of apathy and a label of "poor citizen." More recent discussions of participation have questioned this notion of involvement in the system. Guiseppe Di Palma has noted that voting was only one of various actions making up participation; in addition, he lists discussion, interest, joining an organization, and seeking information as important elements of participation.[1] Marilyn Gittell et al. have written that "middle class criteria, when applied to poor communities are not especially worthwhile. . . . The sad fact is that social scientists have provided too few models of citizen participation applicable to these groups."[2]

That the importance of voting has been overestimated is apparent when one examines participation in New York City's decentralized school districts. The contrasting experiences of Districts 3 and 26 illustrate this sufficiently for present purposes. District 3 in Manhattan includes the communities of Central Park West and Morningside-Manhattanville. Its school population is 81 percent black and Puerto Rican, 18 percent white, and 1 percent Oriental. District 26 in Queens is one of the city's more affluent districts. It includes the Queens areas of Douglaston, Bayside, Fresh Meadows, and the extremities of Flushing. It contains fewer lower-class families than District 3 and is 85 percent white. It is the antithesis of District 3, being predominantly upper middle class. Its schools boast the highest city-wide scores in reading and mathematics.

More people turned out to vote in District 26 than in any other area in the city. Of registered voters, 22 percent voted to select the 9 CSB members from 41 candidates. Only 8.3 percent of the eligible voters in District 3 turned out to select their board from the 35 candidates on the ballot. District 26's CSB is all white, probably due to the fact that few nonwhites voted. This experience was similar in District 3, where the white minority elected six white members to the nine-member board.

What has been surprising, however, is the lack of control the citizens of District 26 have over their board. Although there exists the constant threat that the parents of District 26 may not re-elect this board, on several occasions the community board has not been swayed by community attitudes. Many parents object to the board's position on parochial schools. If any new item is brought before the board, it will not be discussed unless it has been aired at an executive board meeting. Several parents have been openly bitter toward this community school board, complaining that it does as it pleases and disregards the community's wishes.

Although the parents in District 3 did not vote as heavily as those in District 26, they still secured more control over their CSB. In District 3, for example, the overwhelming majority of U.S. Government Title I funds are allocated on a local option basis. Local option programs are designed and developed by the school's Funded Programs Committee and parents. These programs must be approved by the CSB if they conform to federal guidelines and are reasonably designed to meet the educational needs of children eligible for Title I funds. District 3 has recently developed guidelines for school Personnel Practices Committees (PPC's). These committees must include parents from each grade level; representation on them must reflect the ethnic composition of student population. The PPC's are given a large voice in the recruitment and selection of all tax levy and Funded Programs staff, in developing job descriptions and recommending staffing patterns. They may also conduct an on-going evaluation of all staff by visiting classrooms with supervisory personnel.

It is thus clear that voting is not the most important kind of
participation and that it is not directly translatable into influence on
the CSB's. Therefore, the role of important groups in school politics
must be assessed. Here we deal with the church, the UFT, political
clubs, antipoverty agencies, National Economic Growth and Reconstruction Organization (NEGRO) and the Jewish Defense League (JDL);
the role of the various parent groups will be dealt with in Chapter 5.
Although the present rundown of these groups is not comprehensive,
it does suggest the political implications of decentralization referred
to earlier. Before dealing specifically with these groups, a brief consideration of school districting is necessary.

DISTRICTING

In converting the decentralized districts to a city-wide program,
the State Legislature ignored the advantages of smaller districts. The
legislators established districts consisting of a minimum of 20,000
pupils, with most districts containing upward of 30,000 students.

The Bundy Report leaned toward the creation of forty to fifty
districts formed by intermediate and junior high school clusters,
although it also discussed the possibility of either increasing or
decreasing the number further. The exact number and shape of the
new districts were to be determined with great care in order to insure
boundaries that were both educationally sound and socially viable.

The Bundy Report proposed that the determination of these
clusters should take account of such factors as a sense of community,
efficient utilization of school buildings, school feeder patterns, the
number of pupils who would have to transfer from schools they presently attended and the diversity in composition of student population.
The Bundy Report maintained that these criteria would assure school
districts large enough to be educationally viable and avoid the frag-
mentation and economic inefficiency of smaller districts. Another
factor in favor of districts smaller than those prescribed by the
decentralization bill was the demonstration districts, which had shown
that parents can participate effectively in the educational lives of their
children when the school districts are small and manageable.

The law's stipulation that no district may have less than 20,000
pupils in average daily attendance had three important consequences:
the destruction of the demonstration districts, the impossibility for
blacks and Puerto Ricans to develop voting majorities in most cases
and the easy capture of the community school boards by organized
groups.

It seemed obvious to the legislators that to ensure racial harmony
and a workable educational system, all those with an interest in the

outcome should participate in determining the boundaries. The Board
of Education, accordingly, held a series of borough-wide public hearings.
But, circumscribed by legislative limitations of size and time and
baffled by conflicting pressures, it largely preserved existing lines.

Manhattan, however, proved to be an exception. The Board of
Education did redraw its district lines, and some groups protested.
Shortly after the New York City Board of Education completed its
efforts, for example, Puerto Rican parents on Manhattan's Lower
East Side complained that the plan fostered segregation. The Office
of Civil Rights of the U.S. Department of Health, Education and Welfare
investigated these complaints. In April, 1972, the New York Times
reported that J. Stanley Pottinger, the director of the civil rights
office, concluded "that the district boundaries had no actual effect on
the pupil attendance zones of the schools—that while some schools
were placed in different districts, they continued to draw pupils from
the same zones and, therefore, their racial composition was not
affected."[3]

Some groups in Queens have protested the pattern of districting
for other reasons. They had pushed for a district which would combine
the black sections of Districts 27, 28 and 29. They had maintained
that district lines should be drawn on an east-west basis. This would
have created a contiguous black district capable of increasing representation of blacks on the community school board. Their sentiments
were not heeded; district lines were drawn on a north-south basis.
The consequences of this can be discerned by examining the situation
in District 28. In a district with a pupil population 41 percent black
and 6 percent Puerto Rican, the community school board is dominated
by whites from the Forest Hills area. The result was all black schools
and one-way busing of children from south to north.

Certainly the dissatisfaction with the district lines had a damaging
effect on participation in community school board elections and activities. The districting hassle had set the stage for the subsequent
participation of organized groups in school politics.

THE CATHOLIC CHURCH

With the election of 95 CSB members on church slates, the
Catholic church emerged as the single most influential factor in the
1970 school board elections. Because of its unique ties with and its
organizational strength in the community, the church has had an
impact on school elections unmatched by other community groups.
Community persons interviewed in Districts 15 and 25, for example,
indicated that officers of the church actively solicited support for
local Catholic candidates at Sunday services. Their efforts were

frequently supported by smaller but equally vocal Jewish and Protestant parochial interests.

It is not difficult to ascertain the church's interest in the community school boards. The financial plight of parochial schools is well known; they have been forced to close at an ever increasing rate. This has been the case even though the allocation of reimbursable funds to every district provides for a percentage based upon a formula for the parochial schools within its boundaries. The additional financial burden on parents with children in parochial schools has also been publicized. The church understandably desires public assistance to ease this burden and to keep its schools open. Part of its over-all strategy, therefore, has been to support candidates for community school boards who favor this assistance and to use the local boards as a base of political power.

This, indeed, has happened in a few districts. Most often, it took the form of the community school boards' passing a resolution supporting the adoption in the State Legislature of the Lerner Bill. The Lerner Bill would have provided parent-student aid for the education of students in full-time attendance in nonpublic elementary and secondary schools. Such steps have sometimes divided the community from the community school board. In District 25, for example, all the parents interviewed considered this step a crucial turning point in the destruction of any trust for the board by the community. Immediately after CSB 14's endorsement of the Lerner Bill, disruptions broke out, prohibiting further proceedings.

It is remarkable that most church-dominated community school boards made no endorsements of parochial school aid. They evidently feared the rupture such a move might create between the community school board and the community. Some boards, especially those having an almost even split between parochial and nonparochial members, have agreed not to take a public stand on parochial aid. Nonetheless, it has sometimes remained a latent issue, which could arise in the future with explosive force. In District 22, for example, one of the CSB members was accused of conflict of interest because he actively lobbied in the state capitol at Albany for the Lerner Bill. When a Catholic member of CSB 22 resigned filling the vacancy became a church issue. The issue also arose in District 30 over the filling of a board vacancy, resulting in a delay in appointing a successor.

Has the church had an impact on the formulation of other aspects of school policy? Is there a philosophy or orientation to school matters peculiar to Catholic members? The controversial banning of Piri Thomas's book about Puerto Rican life in the city, Down These Mean Streets, by the church-dominated board in District 25 has been attributed to such a "parochial approach." The book allegedly contains "obscenities." At the public meeting to ban the book, all but a few of the parents who spoke were in favor of allowing the book to continue in the schools. Nevertheless, the board voted to ban the book. Although 15 parents took the community school board to court, a New York State supreme court judge held for the local board.

Perhaps the church affiliation of CSB 25's majority somehow affected its decision on this matter, but certainly there is no necessary connection between this affiliation and the decision to ban the book; one need not be so affiliated to question the educational value of a book on grounds of "obscenities."

To get to the bottom of the matter, the performance of CSB 25's parochial majority in other areas must be examined. There is very little community control and parent involvement in decision-making in District 25. On this point, all six individuals (parents and CSB members) interviewed agreed. One member of the board said, "The community should not be involved in tenure—that is a professional question. We have parent observers at principal hiring interviews. Parents can't match my world of experience in professional matters." The parochial members of the CSB have consistently supported this position. It would appear that a common approach to education exists among CSB 25's majority. Nonetheless, one still cannot state conclusively that this approach stems from the church affiliation of these members.

Evidence drawn from other districts indicates that some correlation—but no necessary relationship—exists between a CSB member's church affiliation and a particular approach to aspects of school policy other than support of parochial aid. (We have already seen that even this connection is in no sense usual.) In District 30, for example, church board members often do not vote as a bloc. This experience has been common in several other districts as well. In 5 of the city's 11 church-dominated CSB's (where a majority of the board was elected on a church slate), no bloc voting occurred.

On the other hand, the phenomenon of a church bloc has been apparent in more than half (6 out of 11) such CSB's. Thus a correlation between being elected on a church slate and bloc voting exists. However, it is not overwhelming and in no way entitles one to speak of the pervasive influence of a church philosophy in educational matters.

What are the prospects for the church's future involvement in the city's school politics? This is difficult to assess. In only three districts is there evidence that the church is preparing for the next school board election. A Parochial Parents' Association, for example has been created in District 10 with this object in mind. Whether this lack of activity, city-wide, will characterize the situation in the 1973 elections remains to be seen. It may be that the church will feel that its past efforts have not paid off sufficiently to warrant a repeat performance.

To conclude, the church had an enormous impact on the 1970 school elections; its role in the 1973 elections is in question at this writing. The major impact that church-supported CSB members have had is to back aid to parochial schools. In light of all the recent court rulings against such aid, the effect of such backing has been and perhaps will continue to be minimal. Some bloc voting has occurred on other issues, but we can hardly conclude that it signifies a pervasive and peculiarly Catholic approach to education. Other factors, such as lower middle-class background and conservatism, may more fully explain such activity.

THE UNITED FEDERATION OF TEACHERS

The Old System

The United Federation of Teachers represents about 70,000 teachers and auxiliary pedagogical personnel. It emerged during the 1960s as the most potent educational force in New York City. One reason is that more than 70 percent of the school expense budget has been earmarked for instructional costs, which are controlled in large measure by the union contract. Another reason is that the UFT, since its incorporation in 1960, has taken a larger and larger role in school policy.

Initially, the UFT limited its involvement in school policy to typical trade union demands on wages and working conditions. The latter, because of the peculiar nature of the "educational industry," could be construed as being instrumental to policy. In the early days of the UFT, most of its positions on school policy were negative and successful counters to Board of Education policy. They included, for example, stymieing Board policy to transfer experienced teachers to ghetto schools, opposing school reorganization of junior high schools for integration purposes, and the like. The UFT continued this defensive when it tried to preserve the status quo by opposing the Bundy plan for school decentralization and the three demonstration school districts.

Increasingly, the UFT went on the offensive in developing its strategy to control school policy. Whereas the UFT relied on persuasion to get the Board to adopt its More Effective Schools (MES) plan (a costly compensatory education program that provided saturated services), by the mid-1960s, it successfully negotiated into its contract an educational program based on the MES plan, marking the first time a union had determined educational policy through its contract. Moreover, the UFT sought other policy items—such as the teacher's right to eject disruptive students from the classroom—as bargaining issues. On another front, the UFT helped shape policy by successfully lobbying for a watered-down version of school decentralization in the State Legislature.

The New System

The UFT leadership was antagonistic toward the idea of having to deal with 31 community school boards. Its first move, therefore, after the decentralization bill became an act was to seek as much influence on the CSB's as possible. It became actively involved in the school board elections. A total of 46 CSB members were elected on a UFT slate, placing the union next to the church in terms of impact on the local elections.

The UFT retains its great power in the area of salary scales. Its new contract goes into effect in September, 1972. Binding on the CSB's, it is still negotiated centrally. However, the community boards have a collective bargaining committee of 31 members (one from each board) three representatives of which are on the city Boards negotiating team. The UFT leadership initially resisted this, but, subsequently acknowledged that the CSB role was positive rather than negative. What this change of heart portends for the 1973 elections is hard to say. It could mean a new effort to control the CSB membership and thereby control or influence CSB policy in the next round of negotiations.

Through the budgetary and tenure aspects of the centrally negotiated contract, the UFT is automatically a force to contend with. The CSB's are stringently limited in the vital area of personnel. The UFT contract mandates that teachers not be judged on the basis of performance in the classroom—on whether, for example, they produce students who can read. A tenured teacher may be dismissed only after a complicated grievance process. It is not surprising that so few dismissals have occurred under the present tenure provisions of the UFT contract. Incompetent teachers are protected from the wrath of parents and the CSB's.

The UFT is thus without question a powerful force in all community school districts. One should, however, inquire as to its power in the districts beyond this significant core common to all districts. Our study of the 31 community school districts indicates that the UFT has exerted such power in nineteen districts (1, 2, 9, 10, 12, 13, 14, 15, 18, 21, 22, 23, 25, 26, 27, 28, 29, 30, and 31). The pupil polulation in ten of these districts is predominantly black and Puerto Rican; in the remaining nine it is predominantly white. The CSB's in all but three of the nineteen districts have white majorities.

The union demonstrated its strength in District 26 at two public meetings, on June 24, 1971 and July 22, 1971. At the June meeting the following resolutions appeared on the agenda:

> 17 b—The community Superintendent, through each principal, shall inform the parents associations of the schools concerned of those members of the staff who are beginning their probationary period and those whose probationary period will end during that year.
> 17c—The role of the parent shall be advisory only.
> The parent shall not have a rating responsibility.

The first action of the union-conscious teachers was to get this motion tabled. Some active campaigning for change must have been undertaken, for, at the July meeting, the resolution read as follows:

> 2. Resolved the Community Superintendent, through each principal, shall inform the parent associations of the schools concerned of the status of probation of members of the staff. The parents shall not have a rating responsibility.

Now the separate acts of informing parents and of parents rating teachers were tied together. At the June meeting, informing parents would probably have passed, after which the question of rating could have been independently decided. In July both ideas were linked; so to oppose the idea of parental ratings would also mean no information of who was on probation.

The implied effect of this change illustrates the strength of the union. The UFT's power was further highlighted when the resolution, despite parental protest, was further diluted so that parents will be informed only of a teacher's first and last year of probation. Although several parents and a few board members supported the idea of parental notification of probationary teachers, the majority of both elements had confidence in the ability of the professionals to judge the new teachers.

In some districts the UFT chapter chairman exercises considerable influence. A teacher interviewed in District 1 indicated, for example, that the UFT chairman has met with certain CSB members prior to public meetings. When asked by teachers why such meetings occurred, the UFT representative became defensive and stated that the meetings had nothing to do with his official status as a chapter chairman. This is of particular interest because, as we shall see, several teachers in District 1 have formed the Teachers' Action Caucus (TAC), which is challenging some of the UFT's positions on school policy.

A CSB 25 member stated that the UFT district representative
has actively challenged the CSB on certain matters and refused to
fully cooperate on others. The union initiated grievance proceedings
when the CSB and certain principals decided, for purposes of flexibility
in school program, to increase the size of a few classes by just two
or three students above the UFT contract maximum. On the other
hand, this CSB member indicated that when the UFT was consulted
on the substance of a policy on disruptive children, the union representative showed little interest in the policy except insofar as it
touched upon the union contract; such matters as enlisting the aid of
community agencies on this problem seem of no concern to the UFT
chairman. In this vital area, active UFT cooperation could result in
a more effective program, but it has not been forthcoming.

Sometimes the impact of the union can be discerned in relatively
minor practices and procedures. In District 22, for example, the
CSB chairman manages the public discussions in such a way that professionals are always called on before parents. Although relatively
insignificant in itself, this practice is indicative of the chairman's
philosophy as well as the direction of some of CSB 22's policies.

In District 15, the CSB appointed a committee to evaluate the
district's educational program. The committee consisted of three
Parent-Teacher Association (PTA) presidents, three principals, and
three teachers (including the UFT district chairman). The majority
report of the subcommittee did little more than deal with safe gener-
alities; only the minority report by two of the PTA presidents went
into the procedures that would have to be implemented by each school
if teachers were to be held accountable. One of these procedures was
observation of a teacher by parents—it was recognized that this alone
is not an adequate basis for evaluation, but it is one legitimate and
necessary tool. The CSB appointed three parents (two of whom dissented from the majority report) and two professionals to this committee. This clearly indicates the board's union bias. All of the CSB 15
members interviewed indicated an opposition to parent observation
of teachers on principle: Parents are in no sense trained to evaluate
teachers, the reasoning goes; therefore they should not.

Just such a policy—parent observation of teachers—has been
authorized in Districts 3 and 8, where the UFT is not influential.
The chairman of CSB 8 said that parents have a right to know what
is going on in the classroom and that the CSB was working out procedures to formalize the process. The CSB in District 3 last February
established guidelines for school Personnel Practices Committees
that would permit each school PPC to participate in "an ongoing
evaluation of all staff together with the supervision staff, such evaluation to be based in large measure on visitation and/or participation
by members of the PPC in a set number of classroom periods (to be

determined) and aided by specific criteria which are shared by supervisory staff with parents." The PPC of a school includes parents from
each grade level; representation on the PPC is supposed to reflect
ethnic composition of the student population. Parents have made
classroom visits in both districts 3 and 8.

The UFT has adamantly resisted this practice, calling it
"vigilantism." UFT President Albert Shanker stated that "many of
these visits are done by a self-selected group of parents. It's a kind
of reign of terror here. There have been a number of cases of the
parent-committees using abusive language against the teachers in
front of the students." If the practice is not stopped, says Sandra
Feldman, Shanker's assistant, "it will destroy the educational system
of the city as we know it." Shanker stated that parents were in effect
rating teachers and making recommendations to principals. Many of
these principals were acting principals without tenure, hired by the
same parents who observed teachers. Shanker thus worries that
principals will be obligated to heed the advice of these parents lest
they stand in danger of losing their jobs.[4]

The UFT leadership has recommended that teachers "refuse
to cooperate" with parent committees attempting to observe their
classroom performance. Teachers have been advised to walk out of
classrooms if the principal does not order parents to leave: "To
protest the intrusion all staff members should immediately go to the
school auditorium or cafeteria."[5]

Alfredo Mathew, the community superintendent of District 3,
has referred to this UFT response as "another over-reaction." His
assistant, Clinton Howe, stated that "the union is talking about evaluation, and we're talking about observation. Parents should have the
right to go into the schools to see how their children are being educated.
We don't want chaos. . . . how do we afford parents their rights?" So
long as the principal performs the actual evaluation, officials of
Districts 3 and 8 maintain, the parent observation process cannot
really be abused. Although District 3's guidelines for school PPC's
states "that end-of-year ratings by the principal should consider said
PPC evaluations," no requirement is written in that he agree with
them.[6] To guard against the dangers Shanker feared—acting principals'
being mere rubber stamps for parent observation committees—District
3 included in its guidelines a provision assuring "due process for
staff."

Other districts have also demonstrated their independence of
UFT policies. CSB 4, for example, initiated legal action challenging
the constitutionality of the UFT excessing rules provision (which
result in a "last hired, first fired" situation) with regard to teachers,
because those rules result in de facto discrimination among the
teaching staff. They result in the loss of a significant number of

minority group teachers. This situation has not yet been resolved. A
related legal action in District 3 challenged the UFT excessing provisions on the grounds that dismissing substitutes before regular teachers
would destroy much of the district's educational program. It was
dismissed by the court because it was deemed an "educational" matter
appropriate for the attention of State Commissioner of Education
Ewald Nyquist. Nyquist decided against the CSB.

We have examined some of the challenges to UFT hegemony by
several CSB's. Recently, two teachers' groups have added their voices
to these forces. The African-American Teachers' Association (AATA),
under the leadership of Albert Vann, has charged the UFT and its
allies with attacks against black people's efforts to improve their
schools. In early 1972 it held a convention, attended by some 6,000
black public school teachers. The UFT went to court, charging the
AATA with fostering segregation against white teachers, who were
barred from attending AATA meetings. The group has not as yet had
a significant impact, and it is not likely that it will ever succeed in
altering the policies of the UFT.

A second group is the Teachers' Action Caucus. This group
has sought to make the UFT internally more democratic and refers
to the union's dominance by its president as "Shanker democracy."
TAC has also supported a closer relationship between teachers and
parents than suits the UFT leadership. Shanker's opposition to attempts to make school staffs more reflective of the ethnic backgrounds
of pupils has likewise been attacked by TAC. These are progressive
stances, but TAC has not had an impact on UFT policies. Its resources
are limited, and, in any confrontation with its parent body, it would
be crushed.

TAC's positions on teacher salary and benefits, however, are
very similar to those of the UFT itself. Accordingly, some observers
have questioned the sincerity and significance of TAC's progressive
positions. Its resources are limited and in any confrontation with
its parent body, it would probably be crushed.

POLITICAL CLUBS

In the 1970 school board elections, local political clubs played
a major role—most were Democratic, a few were Republican. Sixteen
community school board members were elected on slates that could
be identified with a political club. They sit on CSB's in seven districts.
Several board members are active in local political clubs. Some have
political aspirations: for example, a former member of CSB 2 ran
for political office and, at present, one member each of CSB's 25 and
28 are running for such office.

Apart from the school elections, the political club has played a significant role in school politics in only one district. This is in District 23, the location of the now defunct Ocean Hill-Brownsville demonstration district. Samuel Wright, local assemblyman and a persistent critic of the experimental district, serves as the chairman of the CSB. He dominates the CSB and can command a majority on almost any issue. Critics have accused him of serving on the board merely to maintain and enlarge his base of political power.

District 23 was the scene of a boycott at the 1970 school board elections. Only 4.9 percent of the registered voters voted in these elections, the lowest turnout in the city. This compares miserably with the 25 percent turnout in the demonstration district elections. What can account for such a vast discrepancy? Many of those who had been active in the demonstration district boycotted the elections to protest its abolition. Furthermore, Wright was able to apply his political skills by removing the names of some of the community control advocates from the ballot on the basis of technicalities. This was perhaps enough in itself to keep many voters home on election day. He was elected by 75 proportional representation votes.

Upon assuming chairmanship of the CSB, Wright was instrumental in removing Nellie Duncan from her post as community superintendent. She was extremely popular, and her supporters maintained that Wright trumped up charges against her because she was too independent to suit his political needs. Since that time, District 23 has had and lost two additional district superintendents. In August, 1971, the CSB under Wright's leadership removed five principals, four of whom had risen to principalship in the original demonstration district. Thus, within a year of assuming office, Wright had succeeded in removing the last vestiges of the demonstration district structure he had so adamantly opposed.

Interviews with community superintendents suggest the chairman's mode of operation. They indicated that the chairman would often insist that expenditure of district funds for unusual matters be approved. The instructions to the community superintendent would be verbal; implicit in them was that his or her job would be in jeopardy if too many questions were asked or approval was not forthcoming. Because instructions were verbal, if the decisions were publicly challenged they could be denied.

Since October, 1971, three sets of charges have been drawn up against Wright by parents and two dissenting CSB members. The substance of these charges is that Wright has abused his powers as board chairman to reward political supporters. For example, the briefs submitted to Chancellor of New York City Schools Harvey Scribner charge that district employees and firms doing business with the district had been required to make "kickbacks" to Wright's

United Political Club. The briefs also alleged that Wright had used
Board of Education money to finance his political activities and that
he had sought city Board leases for buildings owned by officials of
his club. The third charge is that Wright got the CSB to give $500,000
to two security companies "that allegedly falsified vouchers, violated
state and board regulations and the city charter and administrative
code, and exploited guards solely to maximize profits."

The Chancellor has been looking into these charges. What action
he will take is unclear. In the past, he has been reluctant to become
intimately involved in the day-to-day workings of the school districts
lest he set precedents for similar complaints in other districts.
However the situation in District 23 is resolved, it certainly provides
an instance of the impact of political clubs on local school policy.
The charges seem to be too serious to be dismissed by characterizing
them as deriving from the long dispute between Wright and partisans
of the old Ocean Hill-Brownsville demonstration district, as the
assemblyman has claimed. Had the election procedures been more
adequate—simplified requirements to run for office, less complex
voting—this situation might never have developed.

ANTIPOVERTY AGENCIES

The antipoverty agencies have pursued an active role in the
formulation of school policy. What have they accomplished, and how
is it to be assessed?

City-wide, these groups have come together to challenge the
role of the United Parents' Association (UPA) as one of the city's
dominant parents' bodies. Antipoverty interests regard the 400,000-
member UPA as white- and middle-class-oriented and too closely
associated with "establishment" groups in education. Accordingly,
they encouraged the creation of the Community Parents' Association
(CPA) as a counterforce to the UPA.

In the statement announcing the creation of the CPA, it was
pointed out that "It is a feeling of many Black and Puerto Rican parents
. . . that although they represent a majority of the school system, their
voice is not heard" when school policies are determined. It was further
stated that although the UPA was "on the right side" on most issues, it
was "not militant enough." The CPA aims, among other things, at the
repeal of tenure laws for teachers, the abolition of the Board of
Examiners, and the negotiation of union contracts directly with community school boards. It proposed, further, the payment of stipends to
high school students in poverty areas "just as teachers are paid
stipends for additional training in poverty areas."[7]

In response to the formation of the CPA, Blanche Lewis of the UPA stated that the membership of her group was almost half black and Puerto Rican. She questioned the motives of those who created the new group, and suggested that an attempt should have been made to come into the UPA "to supply the militant element they feel is lacking."[8] To date, the CPA has yet to make its influence felt.

Within the school districts, some of the antipoverty groups have sought an active role in school policy. An important item on the agenda of community corporations (which are essentially antipoverty organizations) has been to develop educational programs that take into account the regular educational structures in the district. A draft of prospective educational activities of the Lower East Side Community Corporation, for example, contains the following:

> ---survey existing educational resources within the [Lower East Side] for children and adults . . . ;
> ---begin systematically to analyze resources important for educational change that do not now exist in our community, or are unevenly distributed, and begin working to obtain them;
> ---set up direct contacts with, and constructive support relationships to, all parent associations in the community;
> ---develop systematic information about, and broad personal contacts inside, all public schools in the Lower East Side;
> ---work to create active ties with the main participants in each school—above all, parents, plus students and staff . . . ;
> ---work in cooperation with . . . community groups to build an effective independent district-wide parent-based coalition to deal with broad educational concerns of the Lower East Side community;
> ---work to reopen dialogue and cooperation with the professional staffs of the schools, via the official UFT structure . . . as well as individual teachers or supervisors interested in joint planning or advisory roles with community groups;
> ---strive to develop public school staffs which, in ethnic makeup and in life values, are more representative of the student population of the Lower East Side schools— at all levels, and especially in supervisory roles.

These are some of the specific educational concerns that most community corporations share. Full-time education coordinators are employed to pursue these endeavors.

What impact have the antipoverty agencies had in local school politics? Very few CSB members and parents interviewed mentioned them as participants. Our investigation of the 31 decentralized school districts, however, revealed that they have been a factor in 12 districts (1, 3, 4, 5, 7, 8, 9, 12, 13, 14, 17, and 27). Although only six CSB members were elected on antipoverty corporation slates, since the 1969 elections these agencies in many cases have actively sought to fill board vacancies with people sympathetic to their interests. They have energetically lobbied for teachers, supervisors, and district and local school staffs (coordinators, clerks, and others) more representative of the school system's pupil population.

The demand by community corporations and other groups that CSB's and school personnel be ethnically representative of pupil population has sometimes caused latent ethnic cleavages to burst into the open. Although this has happened in most districts with sizable ethnic minorities, it has been especially pronounced where organized groups—often antipoverty agencies—have actively sought greater representation. The groups involved vary with the make-up of the district—for example, in Districts 1, 6, 13, 14, 15, 27, 28, and 29, it has been blacks and/or Puerto Ricans against whites, whereas in Districts 4, 7, 9, and 19, it has been blacks against Puerto Ricans. Likewise, the intensity of the rivalry has varied; few districts can match the level of hostility in Districts 1, 4, and 14, where the community corporation has been very active.

Parents in District 5 charged their CSB with political favoritism in filling jobs and with job reprisals against employees who dissent against CSB policies. They have appealed to Chancellor Scribner to suspend the board and place the district under a trusteeship. The district superintendent has been dismissed and has indicated that he plans to seek a court order directing his reinstatement. The Haryou Act agency has been implicated in these events because the CSB chairman, who has been charged with "importunities and harassment," is employed as its education coordinator.

The role of the poverty agency in District 14 has also created a stir. The district's former superintendent, who has moved to that office in District 22, has said, "I got tired of fighting the poverty organization and the self-interest groups that were down there. My wife told me I was changing. I didn't like the pressure of feeling, you know, 'Tonight there's a meeting and I hate like hell to go.'"[9]

Because the community corporation in District 4 has perhaps been most successful in terms of its impact on the local school system and has received the most negative publicity, we shall deal with it at length. Our assessment of its activity will apply to a certain extent to those of poverty agencies in other districts as well. Let us begin by briefly noting the composition of CSB 4.

After the 1969 school board elections, CSB 4 was composed of four Puerto Ricans, two blacks, and three whites. One of the board members, a white, resigned almost immediately because of ill health. Another, a priest, resigned in the autumn of 1971 after being assigned a parish outside the district. The East Harlem Community Corporation, with four Puerto Ricans associated with it already on the school board, actively sought to secure a Puerto Rican majority. These efforts were successfully resisted by the blacks and the remaining white on the CSB until February, 1972, when a compromise was worked out that placed the additional Puerto Rican required to secure the pro-community-corporation majority as well as a black on the board. As it stands, the CSB is quite ethnically representative of the pupil population of the district, which is 65 percent Puerto Rican, 33 percent black, and 2 percent white.

The New York Times, on April 26, 1972, criticized the community corporation in an editorial entitled "School Board Turmoil." It is worth quoting because some may view its central point as applicable to the role of the poverty agencies in other districts:

> . . . it is certain that the increasing chaos in East Harlem's District 4 involves, in addition to deliberate disregard of rules and procedures, the flagrant violation of personal rights of parents and the professional rights of administrators. Community members and their children have been threatened. Public board meetings have been disrupted and coerced by special interest groups. The district superintendent, after being denied the right to speak despite the parents' overwhelming demand that he be heard, last week was physically assaulted and had to be escorted by police to safety.
>
> The selection of a highly qualified black professional to the post of deputy superintendent was abruptly rescinded, without regard for the by-laws. The board's policy-making functions are being undermined by improper pressures from outside groups which have exploited and aggravated existing divisions between the black and Puerto Rican sectors. Members of the East Harlem Community Corporation, an antipoverty agency, have brazenly intimidated the community board during its public meetings.
>
> Under such conditions the community atmosphere is poisoned. Administrators, teachers and parents are fearful of reprisals. The education of children is in jeopardy. The stakes, for the community itself and for decentralization in general, are high.[10]

On May 21, 1972, the Times quoted District 4's lame-duck
superintendent as saying, "You get all the blame, and you cannot
make a decision. . . . It's practically impossible to make an administrative decision. . . . When you have to truckle to the community school board, which seems to think your professional integrity
and experience and know-how [are] of no value, then you got to get
out."[11]

The editorial is certainly correct in acknowledging "divisions
between black and Puerto Rican sectors. As Patricia Cayo Sexton
has pointed out, "race and ethnicity underlie much of the open and
hidden conflict in East Harlem, as it always has in the slums of New
York's melting pot."[12] We suggested earlier that these cleavages
frequently accompany attempts to make the personnel of CSB's and
schools more ethnically representative of a district's pupil population.

This explanation underlies much of the ethnic rivalry in District
4. All the CSB 4 members interviewed expressed a desire to move
in this direction—"entrenched groups" (meaning whites), they say,
have far too long dominated their schools. Accordingly, CSB 4 last
summer took legal action challenging the constitutionality of the
excessing provisions of the UFT contract on the grounds that those
rules result in de facto discrimination among the teaching staff.
Likewise, the CSB's majority agrees that supervisory positions
should be filled by as many blacks and Puerto Ricans as possible.
It is only when it must be determined who—a black or a Puerto Rican—
is to fill a position that conflict ensues.

The board's inability to select a deputy superintendent has been
the direct result of this rivalry. Similar difficulties will probably
be encountered when the CSB seeks a replacement for the community
superintendent. On this point the outgoing superintendent's statement
to the Times may have been misleading. He made it sound as if his
removal from office was unexpected, but one of the CSB members
interviewed stated that he (a white) was hired with the understanding
that his contract would not be renewed so that the district could replace him with a qualified black or Puerto Rican.

On one occasion the CSB's commitment to hire more black and
Puerto Rican principals brought it into conflict with its own procedures
for selecting supervisory personnel. In June, 1971, the CSB adopted
procedures that not only provided for the inclusion of parents in the
screening process but also guaranteed that no one could be appointed
as principal or assistant principal who is not acceptable to the representatives of the Parents' Association (PA). PS 171, a predominantly
Puerto Rican school, was pleased with its acting principal, who was
white and wanted him appointed as principal. The CSB, nonetheless,
decided to appoint a Puerto Rican without consulting the PA. Considerable havoc followed this decision, and a public meeting was
disrupted.

The foregoing is an instance of where CSB 4 perhaps too zealously pursued its policy of hiring minority personnel. Likewise, its inability to select a deputy superintendent because of intraboard ethnic rivalry is unfortunate. These particular cases, however, ought not be taken as arguments against the CSB's general policy of hiring qualified persons of minority backgrounds. Although qualified whites can serve the interests of blacks and Puerto Ricans, the view that school boards, school supervisory, and teaching staffs must be ethnically representative of the pupil population of the district if they are to have the necessary ties and identity with the community to be effective certainly has considerable force.

Dr. Kenneth Clark has recently charged that many of the CSB's— and he probably had CSB 4 in mind as a prominent example—are more interested in power and control of patronage than better education. It is certainly possible and appropriate for some purposes to separate concern for quality education from concern for jobs. CSB 4's and the East Harlem Community Corporation's concern for the latter has certainly had its negative effects—it has fostered and enhanced ethnic rivalry already present to a degree. Surely the antipoverty agencies can become self-serving; as Piven and Cloward note, "In many cities the Great Society Agencies became the base for new black and Puerto Rican political organizations whose rhetoric may have been thunderous but whose activities came to consist mainly of vying for position and patronage within the urban political system."[13] We have suggested, however, that there is strong merit in the argument that CSB's and school staffs may be educationally more effective if they are ethnically representative of those they are supposed to serve.

Conflict can be a negative factor. But it can also serve positive functions. Preston Wilcox noted—while he was director of the East Harlem Project, which was founded in 1957—that Puerto Ricans tended to be submissive toward authority while blacks tended to be aggressive toward it.[14] The Puerto Ricans in District 4 no longer are submissive to the degree they once were—the community corporation played an important role in waking them from their apathy. Conflict perhaps contributed to this mightily; as Clinard has said, "The excitement and activity it generates tend to maintain the enthusiasm and support of the slum dweller."[15] The success of the community corporation in District 4, therefore, perhaps owes much to the high level of conflict that has characterized local school politics. Although this conflict has had negative side effects, its positive aspects may in the long run prove to be more important. The push for what some demean as "patronage jobs" cannot be separated from the drive for more effective education, especially in minority districts where white-controlled schools do not work for the children.

GROUPS ACTIVE ON AN AD HOC BASIS

Negro

The National Economic Growth and Reconstruction Organization (NEGRO), headed by Dr. Thomas W. Matthew, is a black self-help group that receives considerable federal funding. It has played a limited though dramatic role in school politics, mainly in District 6.

Construction of new buildings and the utilization of antiquated buildings have been severe problems in this district. Many of the respondents to the question "What are the 5 most important issues in this district?" listed construction of new buildings. One such antiquated structure was PS 186 in District 6. Located on 145th Street, this building was approaching its 80th year of service to the community. Because of the recurrent budget crisis, it was questionable whether 186 would be replaced.

To emphasize the obvious decay of this building, NEGRO moved into the school and shut down the top three floors of the five-story building with the cooperation of teachers and students. Citing unsafe conditions, Matthew enabled the students and staff of 186 to use another facility funded by NEGRO rather than the old building.

CSB 6 had formally asked the appropriate city agencies to include funds for PS 186 in the capital budget, but this move neither expressed the drama nor aroused the enthusiasm of the intervention by NEGRO. Consequently, many in the community viewed the CSB as dragging its feet on this matter; they did not see its response as sufficient, given the magnitude of the problems caused by the decrepit structure.

It is possible that the CSB viewed its action as all that was necessary because NEGRO was there to provide the additional leadership. The fact that the CSB did not provide this leadership perhaps accounts for the negative reaction of much of the community. It might also explain why NEGRO quickly allied itself with the People's Community School Board, an anti-CSB group. In any case, the activities of the CSB faded into the background, and the media only covered NEGRO's efforts.

The Jewish Defense League

The Jewish Defense League (JDL) has been involved in the school politics of District 1. Although the pupil population of that district is 86 percent black and Puerto Rican, the majority of those eligible to vote in school elections are white, and many are Jewish. Whenever

it has perceived the interests of Jews to be threatened, the JDL has
been more than willing to defend teacher interests. A sizable con-
tingent of the JDL turned out at about three meetings in District 1
between January and April, 1972, and altercations erupted between
members of the JDL and some Puerto Ricans. Rumors spread that
the Young Lords, a militant Puerto Rican group, were involved in the
disruption, but little evidence of their presence exists. Indeed, investigation suggests that the Puerto Ricans involved were not organized.

The question remains as to why the JDL was active in District
1. CSB 1 is badly split—one group (three whites) has persistently
defended the autonomy of teachers and fought against a broader role
for parents in the making of school policy; the other group (three
Puerto Ricans and one black) has persistently defended holding teachers
accountable for actual performance and has sought to achieve greater
parental involvement in school planning and programs. Because a
majority of five is required to get anything done, the CSB has been
in stalemate. As long as such a condition obtained, teachers were
not in danger of being held accountable for performance and parents
(mostly black and Puerto Rican) were not likely to secure a greater
role in school affairs.

A threatened break in the stalemate came when Chancellor
Scribner appointed two "trustees" for the sole purpose of enabling
the CSB to fill its two vacancies. Scribner's move meant that there
was no longer hope for a special general election that would surely
have placed two whites on the CSB (recall that most voters in District
1 are white). The "trustee" mechanism would virtually assure a
black and Puerto Rican majority on the CSB. Accordingly, teacher
interests would be threatened; therefore, the JDL was brought into the
Lower East Side school struggle by those whose goals were associated
with the white caucus on the community school board. Simultaneously,
stories had been manufactured as to the racism and violence of
Puerto Ricans; for example, one woman reportedly told City Council
President Sanford Garelik of being threatened with an injection of
heroin if she did not go along with the blacks and Puerto Ricans on
the CSB.

The above suggests the JDL's importance in school politics
and that this role is predicated on a defense of entrenched groups in
the school system.

CENTRAL BOARD POLICY

One of the most important ingredients in educational policy is
personnel. This judgment affirms the projection of several analysts
of decentralization that "the effectiveness of the local school board
in changing the schools will depend to a great extent on the cooperation and proficiency of the school staff in carrying out such
changes."[1] One can argue, further, that, if the community school
district is bound by existing personnel practices, including central
examination and assignment of staff, its power base will not have
broadened in the crucial area of control over jobs.

The deficiencies of the New York City school personnel system
have prompted studies by city commissions, universities, civic
associations, and the Board of Education for 25 years. The need for
reforming personnel practices and procedures in New York City
schools was identified early.

The areas of greatest concern to social scientists studying the
school system have been the recruitment and selection procedure;
in-service training and supervision; the promotion and examination
process; the procedure for evaluation of personnel; and the inbred
nature of the entire personnel system.

In an extensive study of the New York City schools conducted
in 1951 George Strayer and Louis Yavner found supervision poor,
guaranteeing tenure to almost all teachers as a matter of course
rather than as a reward for competence. They concluded, "Any view
that an examining board exists primarily to keep out of the system
incompetent persons who might have obtained employment under a
political spoils system is several decades behind modern thinking
in public personnel administration."[2]

24

Strayer and Yavner felt that supervisory personnel should have the authority to control their own schools, to assess community needs, and to organize, administer, and supervise the schools in order to meet those needs. They should be given ample latitude in formulating and implementing in-service training programs and workshops for their teachers, using local talent or specialists.

In their 1960 study, Wallace Sayre and Herbert Kaufman determined that the New York City Board of Education had little say in personnel matters, because

> the controls issued from Albany in state law and rules developed largely under the influence of the leaders of the teachers' organization bind the discretion of the Board to procedures and policies the leaders of the teachers prefer. If they cannot move the Board to take all the action the teachers want, they can achieve their alternative goal; the Board is immobilized in any effort to move in directions the leaders of the teachers strongly resist.[3]

A study by Daniel E. Griffiths et al. in 1963 recommended a thorough examination of the role of the Board of Examiners that would focus on the validity of the testing procedures, the tests themselves, and the outcome of the testing.[4] In 1966, Griffiths and his research team at New York University updated their study. They reported bureaucratic inefficiencies in recruitment and promotion procedures, commented on the outmoded nature of the examination system and on the favored position of insiders. They recommended creation of an entirely new personnel system.[5]

Since 1967, rising ghetto hostility toward teachers and principals has provided the major impetus for changing the system. A study of ghetto parents by the Center for Urban Education in 1967 concluded that they perceived principals and teachers to be the key factors in the educational performance of their children. They wanted powers to fire those teachers and principals they deemed incompetent. The whole community control movement, beginning with the 1967 Intermediate School (IS) 201 boycott, stressed the need to establish accountability of school professionals.

The IS 201 boycott was the turning point. Within a year, more than a dozen parental boycotts in the ghettos hinged on the removal of a principal. As a result of pressure from parents in ghetto areas, three experiments on local control were instituted in 1967 by the Board of Education as demonstration districts. The experiments were evaluated by the Institute for Community Studies over a three-year period. Participant-observers reported that the one common

complaint public school parents have against the schools concerned
school personnel; they wanted to hold teachers and supervisors
accountable.

The institute's study of the three demonstration districts documents the frustration of local boards in recruiting personnel. In
particular, the boards and administrators of Ocean Hill-Brownsville
and IS 201 believed that selection of their own personnel was crucial
to the success of the experiment.[6] They were aware that a majority
of New York City supervisors were hostile to the intent of the projects
for fear of encroachment on their civil service status. In desperation,
the demonstration districts pressured the State Education Commissioner to grant the creation of a new job category, "demonstration
school principal," which by-passed traditional city civil service
procedures. Over the three-year course of the experiments, 13 of
the principals were selected by the unit administrators and the boards
in Ocean Hill-Brownsville; 4 of the 8 principals were chosen in IS
201, and 2 of the 6 principals in Two Bridges. New York City had,
for the first time, via the demonstration districts, a substantial
number of minority personnel, including the first black superintendent
and black, Puerto Rican, and Chinese principals.

THE COMMUNITY BOARDS AND PERSONNEL

For most of the three years of the experiments, New York
City experienced a traumatic conflict over the community control
issue. The conflict reached into the state legislature, which found
it almost impossible to resist the well-organized campaign of school
professionals to retain protection for their jobs. Thus, the 1969
decentralization act avoided transferring of substantial personnel
power to the local communities. The legislation retained the city-
wide examination system, though diluted for supervisory appointments. It maintained most teacher hiring as a central function and
provided for local hiring in districts where schools scored in the
lowest 45 percent of reading achievement.

Frustrated by the state legislature's refusal to undermine the
power of the Board of Examiners, the Legal Defense and Educational
Fund of the National Association for the Advancement of Colored
People (NAACP) filed a suit in 1970 in federal court challenging the
board's testing procedures. The NAACP charged that central testing
procedures were discriminatory and violated the New York State
Constitution's requirement that all public appointments be made on
the basis of "merit and fitness." The brief pointed to the small
percentage of minority personnel (compared to other cities) in a
school system with a majority of minority students. (See Table 2.)

TABLE 2

Comparison of Percentage of Black and Puerto Rican
Principals to White Principals in Five Largest
U.S. School Systems, 1970

City	Total Number of Principals	Percent Black	Percent Puerto Rican	Percent Black and Puerto Rican[a]
Detroit	281	16.7	—	16.7
Philadelphia	267	16.7	—	16.7
Los Angeles	1,012	8.0	1.7	9.7
Chicago	479	6.9	—	6.9
New York	862	1.3	0.1	1.4

City	Total Number of Assistant Principals	Percent Black	Percent Puerto Rican	Percent Black and Puerto Rican
Detroit	360	24.7	0.2	24.9
Philadelphia	225	37.0	—	37.0
Los Angeles	—	—	—	—
Chicago	714	32.5	—	32.5
New York	1,610	7.0	0.2	7.2

[a]Thus New York City has by far the lowest percentage of minority representation. The next lowest city, Chicago, has almost five times the percentage of minority principals found in New York City. As is shown also in the table above, there is a similar imbalance of minority assistant principals.

Source: Chance and Mercado v. Board of Education, 330 Federal Supplement (S.D. New York, 1971).

The Community District Superintendent

The 1969 law made one major change in personnel policy under decentralization, by calling for the appointment of the local community superintendent (formerly the district superintendent) by the local

community school board. Earlier studies of field or district superintendents had demonstrated their generally minimal role in the
development of school policy in the district. The headquarters bureaucracy controlled almost all aspects of educational decision-making
and left little to the discretion of the district superintendent. District
superintendents did not function as an effective liaison between professional headquarters staff and the local school district. If decentralization was to be effected even in a limited way, the role of the
local superintendent had to be changed.

The decentralization act of 1969 (Section 2590-e pt. 1) provided
that "each community board shall employ a community superintendent
by contract for a term of not less than two nor more than four years,
subject to removal for cause, at a salary to be fixed within the
budgetary allocation therefor, subject to the provisions of subdivision
two of section twenty-five hundred ninety-j of this article." The
method of appointment was changed, but the authority and responsibility
of the office were more clearly detailed.

2590-f. Powers and Duties of
Community Superintendents

Except as otherwise expressly provided in this
article, under the direction of his community board,
each community superintendent shall have:

a. the same powers and duties with respect to the
schools and programs under the jurisdiction
of his community board as the superintendent
of schools of the city district of the city of New
York had on the effective date of this article;
and

b. the power to delegate any of his powers and
duties to such subordinate officers or employees
of his community board as he deems appropriate
and to modify or rescind any power so delegated.

In exercising such powers and duties each community
superintendent shall comply with all applicable provisions of law, by-laws, rules or regulations, directives
or agreements of the city board, the chancellor and his
community board and with the educational and operational policies established by the city board and his community board.

Essentially, it was intended that the community superintendent would enforce the policy directives of the CSB. But, with minimal formal guidelines, the actual relationships among the community superintendent, the CSB, and the community would depend to a large extent on the personality and orientation of the community superintendent and the particular characterization of the local board and the neighborhood.

About 61 percent of incumbent superintendents were automatically reappointed for the minimum two-year contract period after the school board elections in 1970. The selection of 14 new community superintendents in that first period did not demonstrate any departure from the traditional kinds of candidates, except in one district. In all other cases, people who met the traditional requirements of the system were chosen. The lack of time (75 days to the new school year) and experience was instrumental in fostering a cautious approach. This initial thrust was, however, to have significant consequences for most districts during their first two years of operation.

SELECTION PROCEDURES

It is of interest to look at the procedures adopted by those boards who had to recruit new superintendents. Some chose to confine the activity to their membership; others relied on groups (particularly parents) within the community. In most cases initial efforts included advertisements in educational journals and newspapers.

District 6 in Manhattan originally established a mechanism for community participation. As reported by the board's former president, the procedure involved the following five steps:

1. The board advertised for the job in The New York Times and educational journals. Almost 100 applications were received.

2. A parent-community screening panel to rate each applicant was selected. This panel was made up of one representative from each of three planning areas in the district. This made a panel of 6 community representatives and 13 parents.

3. Of the applicants, 14 were rated excellent by this panel.

4. Together with the CSB, the panel next narrowed the group down to three individuals.

5. The CSB then selected one of these individuals to be the community superintendent.

Other districts utilize parents and the community as observers and advisers but do not permit them to vote on candidates. The September 1971 public meeting in District 26 approved the following resolution outlining a procedure for parent involvement in the selection process:

> RESOLVED that the Community School Board shall convene a meeting of presidents of parent associations of schools under its jurisdiction, at which meeting three representatives shall be chosen, with each school having one vote, to observe interviews with those applicants whom the Community School Board deems most qualified. The Community School Board shall convene a meeting of presidents of the parents associations of the public high schools in the District, at which meeting one representative shall be chosen, with each school having one vote, to observe interviews with those applicants whom the Community School Board deems most qualified. The Community School Board shall convene a meeting of representatives of community, civic and youth organizations from a list approved by the Community School Board, at which meeting one representative shall be chosen, with each group having one vote, to observe interviews with those applicants whom the Community School Board deems most qualified. BE IT FURTHER RESOLVED that the five observers chosen above may submit questions in advance which they would like asked of the applicants during the interviews, but shall not ask questions of the applicants. After the applicants have been interviewed, the observers shall make a recommendation, which shall be advisory only.
>
> RESOLVED that the Community School Board shall continue deliberations with the final responsibility in the selection continuing to rest in the Community School Board.

Later, District 26 amended these provisions to include participation by the CSA and the UFT:

> RESOLVED to amend the Policy and Procedures for Selecting a Community Superintendent as follows: The number of observers at interviews conducted by the Community School Board shall be increased by two and these shall be (1) the head of the C.S.A. in the District or a designee and (2) the District U.F.T. representative or a designee.

During that first period, most community school boards did not view parent involvement in the selection of the community superintendent

as essential. But that may change, as 18 of the 31 districts begin to
look for replacement candidates for the 1972-73 school year. At least
some of the pressure for change was a result of conflict of interest
between the community superintendent and the community and/or the
CSB. In a number of districts parents and school board members
expressed concern with the lack of openness of the community superintendent. Board members as a group felt less intimidated by the
superintendent. In response to questionnaires on this issue, more
than half the parents interviewed stated that the community superintendent made information difficult to get. (See Table 3.) When the
community superintendent is selected without parent involvement,
parents and community activists within a local school district may not
have equal access to the superintendent and consequently disagree in
their judgments. Opposition groups are more likely to feel—and
actually be—closed out. Very few of the superintendents have made
a concerted effort to keep community groups informed by meeting with
them on a regular basis; most rely on regular community school
board meetings to make information public.

SUPERINTENDENT-CSB RELATIONS

Many districts have run into problems between board members
who were looking for educational change and superintendents content
to work within the framework of a centralized system. In some
cases, this led to conflicts in authority between the board and the
superintendent. Although this situation has been more prevalent in
areas with large minority school population, white districts have also
been affected: Districts such as 31 in Staten Island (87 percent white;
9 white board members), 26 in Queens (85 percent white; 9 white board
members), and 21 in Brooklyn (81 percent white, 9 white board
members) all reported some problems. Conflicts between community
school boards and superintendents were also a product of political
conflicts in the initial struggle to establish board supremacy. In at
least two black districts, this was not a black-white conflict but a
personal political battle for control waged by individual board members.
The local school district was seen as an important political resource
too valuable to leave to a school professional.

In some districts it is the community superintendent who has
established supremacy. A CSB member in District 7 in the South
Bronx, referring to the community superintendent, cites one prime
reason for the breakdown in his district: "He [the district superintendent] does not follow our suggestions . . . he makes up the law."
The president of the board agrees, claiming the community superintendent doesn't keep the board informed on important matters and

TABLE 3

Openness of Community Superintendents

	"Community Superintendent Kept Me Well Informed" (in percent)	"Community Superintendent Made Information Difficult to Get" (in percent)
Parents	42.8	57.2
Board members	77.0	23.0

Sources: Answers to questionnaire; interviews.

proceeds on his own. Members of the community interviewed agreed that the only programs adopted by this board are those favored by the community superintendent. This pattern is repeated in District 21 in South Brooklyn. "We've done nothing. We don't run this district," one board member stated when speaking of the community superintendent. This superintendent, similar to the one in District 7, has been reluctant to utilize any of the plans of the committees of her school board. She works as she did under the centralized system, ignoring programs she doesn't approve of; she is often secretive and in general has prevented the community board from bringing any meaningful changes in educational policies.

One of the essential elements to be tested in decentralization is whether professional and lay interests can be balanced in the decision-making process. Will community school board-community superintendent relations change because of the new selection process, and, if so, what impact will this have on political and educational outputs? Certainly the first two-year period is too early to make any meaningful judgment. First, as was noted, almost all the boards retained their district superintendents; second, changes in the recruitment process and the kinds of candidates chosen cannot be expected to occur quickly. The full impact of local board selection of superintendents must await at least another two to four years to determine any change in who is selected and then an additional period for observed changes in CSB-community superintendent relations and their impact on educational program and output.

Dr. Kenneth Clark, an early supporter of decentralization, shocked many of its enthusiasts (and pleased its protagonists) by a statement in the spring of 1972 condemning the political intrigue of the local boards and the lack of attention to educational issues. His concern

was with those board members who are solely interested in the local
boards as a power base. It would be foolish to presume that intensi-
fication of local politics would not be a part of the decentralization.
The real question is the extent to which it serves the educational
output. Although Clark's warning is useful, it is far too early to draw
hard and fast conclusions. Distinctions between boards is a necessary
part of any evaluation. Why, for example, is CSB 23 so vulnerable to
a wholly political (party) orientation, while other boards are not?
Can such an orientation be redirected?

PRINCIPALS

Most educators concede that the over-all educational level and
the tone and climate of the schools depend on the principal. Dale
Mann has said that "building principals participate in, and affect,
decisions about every single aspect of education at the local level."[7]
In a study of high school principals in New York City, Arthur Vidich
concludes:

> It obviously is not a system to encourage and reward the
> innovative or the critical. This is not to say, however,
> that it does not select competent men. It is that compe-
> tence is oriented almost entirely toward mastering the
> tasks, definitions of problems, and the rhetoric of the
> established system. And the examination system is of
> course administered by men who are a product of it: the
> Board of Examiners. [8]

The 1969 Decentralization Law left the selection of the principal
under the control of the Board of Examiners, with two changes:

> 1. It shifted the authority for appointing supervisory
> personnel for elementary, junior high, and intermediate
> schools from the central Board to the community school
> boards.
> 2. It eliminated the procedure of ranking personnel
> after they had passed the qualifying examination. In-
> stead, all persons named on the lists were considered
> "qualified" for appropriate available positions, and com-
> munity boards could appoint the person they found best
> suited for the job from anywhere on the lists.

The system of examinations remained intact, however. A candidate
was eligible for placement on a qualifying list only if he first met

the Board of Education requirements which included passing the
appropriate examination administered by the Board of Examiners.
The retention of the Board of Examiners was a blow to minority group
parents who wanted the power to select supervisory personnel. Some
studies indicated that a significant outcome of the examination system
was the negligible amount of Black and Puerto Rican professionals in
the New York City school system. For example, in the Griffiths study
published in 1963, it was stated: "However, as one examines the data
in detail, it does seem that Negro staff members of the New York City
Public Schools may have been less mobile than others, geographically
among the districts and hierarchically up the system's promotional
ladder."[9]

Just before the newly elected community boards took office, all
persons on the eligible list for elementary school principal approved
by the central Board received appointments to the title and salary of
elementary school principal, in accordance with the law. Former
City Council President Francis X. Smith had urged the Interim Board*
as "its first order of business to find places for some fifty principals
who are wasted in routine chores."[10]

The 106 individuals on the elementary school principal eligibility
list who were automatically appointed on March 31, 1970 as "auxiliary
principals" have yet to be placed in elementary school principal
vacancies. Most of these "auxiliary principals" are serving as
elementary school assistant principals or are stationed in junior high
schools.

Thus, the 1969 Decentralization Law opened a new direction in
the old debate over personnel. It gave the community school boards
the responsibility for making supervisory appointments for the schools
under their jurisdiction and changed the function of the Board of
Examiners in preliminary screening. And, in the absence of a new
eligibility list, community boards were able to select as "interim
acting principals," individuals who met state certification and had
some experience or training. And, in fact, this was the policy set
forth by the Interim Central Board.

This circumstance offered the CSB's an opportunity to experiment
in the appointment of principals. Although most of the boards continued to use personnel previously licensed by the Board of Examiners,
a few boards chose supervisory personnel with state accreditation
who had not met the special requirements of the New York City Board
of Examiners. Those community school boards tended to be in

---

*"Interim Board" refers to the five-member central Board of
Education, set up as part of the 1969 decentralization act.

districts with large minority population and they sought out more black and Puerto Rican candidates. For example, Districts 9, 10, and 13 actively recruited minority supervisors. As of spring, 1971, of a total of 108 principals appointed by community school boards, 45 were minority. This strategy was also used in District 3.

The "interim acting principal" option answered the problem of putting a man in charge who the community and the CSB thought was the most competent whether or not he met the requirements of the Board of Examiners. Many CSB members stated that they often found that holders of licenses from the Board of Examiners did not possess the ability to perform the duties of a supervisory position for which they were licensed.

In 1971, School Chancellor Harvey Scribner, testifying about the examination process, at the Hearings of the City Commission on Human Rights, called it " . . . antiquated, outmoded, and inconsistent with both contemporary educational requirements and the concept of de-centralized schools."[11] Most damaging was the testimony of Dr. Theodore Lang, then Deputy Director of Personnel for the Board of Education, that the Board of Examiners operates without clear criteria and remains the sole judge of content and performance; that there are no job descriptions to pass on to the Department of Personnel; and that appointments are not challenged by the Chancellor.

The Mansfield Decision

Thus, the minority group principals selected by community school boards were in a tenuous position. It was only a matter of time before the Board of Examiners would give a new examination and issue a new elementary school principals eligibility list. (Section 2573 of the State Education Law provides that normally all vacancies must be filled with-in six months by appointment from an appropriate list.) And some of the minority principals felt they would not receive their licenses from the Board of Examiners because of discrimination. Community boards, in turn, felt that their new flexibility of appointment was short lived.

It was this circumstance that provoked the NAACP Legal Defense Fund, on behalf of Acting Principals Louis Mercado of District 3 and Boston Chance of District 1, to bring suit against the Board of Examiners and the Board of Education on the ground that the examination was discriminatory (Chance had failed the examination and Mercado refused to take it). The plaintiffs argued:

Were it not for New York City's special examination and licensing procedure, plaintiffs Chance and Mercado would have been certified by the state for the position, and

both are specially trained to be principals, having
graduated from a year-long Fordham University Instructional Administrators and Principals Internship
Program in Urban Education.[12]

Judge Mansfield found in favor of the plaintiffs, concluding that the
evidence reveals that "the examinations prepared and administered
by the Board of Examiners for the licensing of supervisory personnel,
such as Principals and Assistant Principals, have the de facto effect
of discriminating significantly and substantially against Black and
Puerto Rican applicants."[13] Subsequently, Judge Mansfield charged
the Board of Examiners "to consider an overhaul that will not eliminate
racial discrimination, but lead to procedures that will be more
adaptable to the Community School Board type of administration."[14]
A temporary restraining order is presently in effect which forbids
the Board of Examiners from promulgating any new eligibility lists
until new performance-based criteria are developed. Thus, though an
examination for elementary school principals was held on November
3, 1970, the issuance of a new list on the basis of this examination
has been enjoined under Judge Mansfield's order.[15]

Community school districts are currently operating under interim
procedures adopted by the Board of Education. These procedures
permit community school boards to hire candidates who are eligible
for the examination under the former New York City procedures or who
meet state certification standards. Newly appointed supervisors will
not receive tenure. (Through amendment of the Education Law at the
1971 session of the state legislature, tenure for supervisors was
abolished.) However, those who already have tenure will retain it.

The Law provided for two hiring and assignment processes: a
basic method which applies uniformly to teaching and supervisory
personnel and an alternate method which applies only to teachers and
which community boards may employ only under certain circumstances.*

According to the basic method, all candidates hired will have to
meet minimum education and experience requirements (not less than
state certification requirements) established by the chancellor. All
candidates, except those for the position of chancellor, executive
deputy, deputy, and assistant superintendent, must be examined and
placed on eligibility lists by the Board of Examiners.

---

*An alternate method may be used by community boards to obtain
personnel for any school which is ranked in the bottom 45 percentile of
a city-wide reading test given annually.

TABLE 4

Sampling of Districts: Principals
Appointed by Community School Boards, 1970-71

Borough	District	School	Unlicensed Principal	Licensed Principal	Total
Manhattan	2	PS 2, 190, 198, JHS 167	4		4
	3	IS 44, PS 76, 84, 145	4		
		PS 75		1	5
	4	IS 13	1		1
Bronx	7[a]	PS 1, 37, 49, 149	5		
		PS 124		1	6
	8[a]	PS 62, 119, 125, 138, 232	6		
		PS 48, 93, 107		3	9
	9[a]	PS 114, 126, 132	5		5
	10	PS 46, 56, 95		3	3
	11	PS 68, 89, 121		3	3
	12[b]			3	3
	13	PS 67		1	1
Brooklyn	17[b]		3		
				4	7
	10	PS 115, 219, 233	3		
		PS 244		1	4
	20[b]			4	4
	21	PS 41, 97		2	2
	22	JHS 234, 278, IS 14		3	3
Queens	24	PS 119, JHS 125		2	2
	25	PS 29, 164, 201, 219, JHS 154, 163, 168, 184, 218		9	9
	26	PS 162, 178, 188, 205, 221, JHS 67		6	6
	27	PS 96, 106, IS 53		3	3
Staten Island	31	PS 118, 131, 135, 156	1	11	12

[a]All school numbers not available.
[b]School numbers not available.

Source: Interviews with CSB members and CSB district office.

TABLE 5

Principals Appointed by Community School Boards,
September, 1970-September, 1971[a]

	Elementary Day	Junior High	Total
Acting Principals	85	23	108

Minority Principals Appointed by Community School
Boards, September, 1970-September, 1971[a]

	Elementary Day	Junior High	Total
Acting Principals	35	10	45

[a]Latest information the New York City Board of Education
would release.

Source: Director of Personnel for the Board of Education,
New York City.

The Board of Examiners is continued in substantially its traditional role except for a few minor adjustments. Although the chancellor may serve as a member of the Board of Examiners, he can
never be chosen as chairman under the new rotating chairmanship
system. Ranking is continued for the filling of teacher vacancies,
although it is abolished for supervisory positions.

One of the hoped-for changes under decentralization was the
involvement of parents in the selection of school principals, but the
law provided only for "meaningful consultation." That phrase has
been interpreted differently in various districts throughout the city.

The PA at PS 222 in District 22 brought suit against its local
board contending that it was presented with "the choice of one candidate" and asked that the board be directed to remove the appointee
until there has been "meaningful consultation." The PA assumed it
should have a role and pressured for representation in decision-
making. The state supreme court dismissed the case indicating that
the law does not require a parental role. The chairman of the District
22 school board noted that it was "unwarranted to think we haven't
considered parent consultation. We tried to persuade the parents
that consultation does not mean a veto over our judgment."

TABLE 6

Selected Principal Vacancies, June, 1972

District	Number of Vacancies
1	11
2	1 (PS 6)
4	2
5	1 (PS 175)
6	0
8	4
10	2 (PS 26, JHS 143)
11	0
12	3
13	0
15	0
17	1
19	1 (PS 260)
23	3
24	2
25	0
26	4
28	1

Source: Interviews at CSB offices

Most districts (19 of them) have given a narrow interpretation to "meaningful consultation," allowing parents to be present at interviews but not permitting them to question the candidate. Where the parents feel the board will operate in their interest, there is little resistance. In Districts 25, 26, 27, and 31 parents are invited to interviews for principals but sit apart from the board and the applicant. All queries are made by the board members. At the conclusion of the meeting, parents may express their opinions as to the candidates interviewed; but in no way is a PA decision binding on the board. Principals hired in these districts have not been challenged by parents.

PA Present at Interview Can't Question			PA on Committee Conducts Interview, Gives Board 3 Names	
Districts			Districts	
1	7	11	3	6
2	10	12	4	8

PA Present at Interview Can't Question			PA on Committee Conducts Interview, Gives Board 3 Names	
Districts			Districts	
13	22	27	9	19
16	23	28	15	20
18	25	29	17	24
21	26	30		
		31		

Only 29 percent, 9 community school boards, actually have instituted meaningful consultation with parents. Several of the districts listed in the first column above have informal mechanisms by which they grant parents access to decision-making. This has taken the form of verbal communication between members of a PA and members of a school board. Some board members in several districts have noted that they consult with selected parents in the area. This arrangement is at best temporary, subject to the whim of the community school board and its members. Nonetheless, its importance should not be underestimated.

The districts with structured involvement all work with various modifications of the following procedure:

1. Advertisement of vacancy.
2. Acceptance of applications.
3. Committee screening of applicants to a final group of 11 candidates (committee's composition varies from only CSB members to only PA members).
4. Interviews of 11 candidates handled by school PA.
5. PA presents 3 names to CSB for final selection.

In most districts this procedure has functioned well; it has accounted for the selection of more than 25 principals. District 6 selected five principals through this method. In each instance the CSB selected the first choice of the PA. However, in one school, the PA selected two men for the position of principal. The legal problems surrounding pay and designation were agreed to by the men involved, before the parents presented their idea at a public meeting in November. The board, however, refused to consider the matter at the time that the parents wanted it discussed. The PA was infuriated by this action and refused to allow the meetings to continue. The board declared that it would discuss the issue when the agenda called for that subject. With both sides unwilling to compromise, the meeting broke up. The failure to compromise gave the community the impression the board was disregarding its position. The CSB viewed the action as another unreasonable demand. This might suggest to some that, if parents

are encouraged to participate, expectations will be raised and demands increased.

Even in the districts that have used consultation, the final power
to appoint is still retained by the community school board, a fact that
has aroused much opposition. The more vocal communities continue
to pressure the boards to accept their recommendations although
the boards are not legally required to do so.

In the appointment of principals the CSB's have been quite
active, hiring 153 new people in the first year of decentralization.
Designations have continued and by September, 1972 as expected
approximately 300 new principals had been selected. This represents
a turnover of one-third the principals in the city. At a minimum the
impact appears to be directly related to minority-group representation: close to 100 of those principals selected are black and Puerto
Rican. A sampling of 14 districts shows that districts with a majority
of white CSB members continue to select licensed principals.

It does not appear that many of these new principals are demon-
strably different from their predecessors. Those selected under a
screening process involving parents are probably more community-
oriented, an asset considered by Keith Goldhammer to be essential
to good school administration. But the CSB's seem reluctant to stray
from the traditional types of school professionals, and it is therefore
unlikely that new principals will be any more innovative than the
people they replace. A more comprehensive long-range study of
principals who do not have traditional credentials matched against
a control group of those with credentials would be necessary to
demonstrate any meaningful differences. Certainly the selection of
more minority-group principals should have some impact on attitudes
and learning environment in schools to which they are appointed; we
have seen evidence of this. These principals, however, claim that
they are limited in what they can do in a school by the constraints
of the budget and the union contract and because they cannot screen
staff.

TEACHER SELECTION AND RECRUITMENT

Testimony by Dr. Jay Greene of the Board of Examiners at the
City Commission on Human Rights hearings revealed little change
in the teacher recruitment and selection process described by Daniel
Griffiths in 1963 and 1966. Of teachers in the New York City public
school system, 90 percent are trained in a New York City college—
65 percent of them at one of the colleges of the City University of
New York (CUNY), up 5 percent since 1963.

Upon completion of the required course of study, graduates are qualified to teach according to state standards but not according to city standards. As the Bundy Report notes, "The only way one can be licensed to teach in the New York City school system is to pass an examination. This is in contrast to the procedure in other districts, urban and suburban, where the entrance doors for a candidate consist only of state certification requirements and a personal interview."16

At the classroom level there are two teacher categories: regular and substitute. Regular teachers are those who have met all requirements and passed a regular teacher-licensing examination. Permanent substitutes (as distinguished from per-diem substitutes) have full-time continuous classroom responsibilities in one school; they are not fully qualified and have not met all requirements but have passed a less demanding substitute's examination. In February 1969, the Board of Education stopped issuing permanent substitute licenses, in response to pressure by parents and the UFT. The teacher shortage was over. The Board encouraged its substitutes to obtain regular teaching licenses. In June 1970, the Board announced plans to drop 2,000 full-time substitutes.

The severest criticism of the substitute license is its elimination of the requirement for student teaching. The student teaching experience has been likened by educators to the internship in medicine. Despite New York City's special examination requirements, which have been justified by the need for high standards as of 1967, most regular teachers have entered the system as substitutes.*

TEACHER TRAINING

Testimony at hearings of the City Commission on Human Rights also brought out criticisms of colleges and universities for "pushing through" most teacher candidates, whether or not they are competent in subject matter. And, on their part, officials from central headquarters of the Board of Education testified that college records are not used by examiners.

Although programs in the city colleges vary widely, the typical teacher candidate receives a baccalaureate degree that includes 24

---

*The 1967 Griffiths study indicated that one-third of all teaching positions were filled by substitutes. When the figures for all positions were broken down, the primary route to high school teaching was by substitute license. That figure has since declined to 12-15 percent.

semester hours in the professional study of education and a college-supervised student teaching experience. Table 7 shows a sample of CUNY colleges and the required hours of student teaching. As the table indicates, the education sequence has remained the same for years. All schools offer student teaching in the final year. For most prospective teachers this is their first professional contact with children. Student teaching assignments are in no small measure based on travel convenience for both student and supervisor. But teacher preparation is far removed from the classroom experience, especially in the urban school. As Dr. John Fisher, president of Columbia Teachers College has observed, "Academic training, though essential, is not sufficient. Understanding of the people with whom one works, understanding of the situations from which those people come, is at least equal in importance to possession of the traditional types of academic and systematized professional preparation."[17]

Recently, several of the city colleges have introduced experimental programs that minimize traditional course work, requiring that students spend most of their time in the field working with children. Clearly, a root cause of the problems in relations between middle-class teachers and poor students has been the training and educational background of teachers. For years, the ghetto schools have been understaffed largely because teachers who passed the examination and were licensed to teach in the city simply did not want to teach in the ghetto areas and thus either refused assignments to schools they regarded as difficult[18] or transferred from these schools as soon as possible. In an earlier study, David Rogers concluded, "The city colleges have not only failed to play a role as change agents, they have actively obstructed school reform by failing to revamp their teacher training courses in light of the vast demographic and socio-economic changes in the city in recent decades. They are almost as responsible for the schools' failures as are board officials, since they trained most of these officials."[19]

IN-SERVICE TRAINING

In Daniel Griffiths's study, mentioned earlier, the majority of teachers who were planning to leave the school system complained of no orientation on their first assignment. This was deemed the most significant factor in causing bewilderment and job dissatisfaction. Griffiths found the Board of Education's role in orientation negligible. There was an absence of in-service courses and standardized information. Also few principals played an active role in the professional development of teachers. Only twelve teachers from a staff of 60,000 had been dismissed over a six-year period.

TABLE 7

Student Teaching in the City University of New York, 1971-72

College	Student Enrollment Elem.	Sec.	Number of Semesters Elem.	Sec.	Year of Student Teaching	Number of Hours of Student Teaching Elem.	Sec.	How Long Program Has Been in Effect	Number of Credits Given for Student Teaching Elem.	Sec.
Brooklyn College	724 per semester	325	2	1	Senior	Min. 325	Min. 180	Since 1950s	7	7
City College	375 per semester		2	1	Senior	Min. 300	Min. 225	Many years	6 plus	6
Hunter College	132 per semester	146	1	1	Senior	Min. 300	Min. 120	Many years	4	3
Lehman College	700 per year		1	1	Lower or upper senior	Min. 300	Min. 120 198-240 college require.	Many years	4	3
Queens College	1,000 per year		1	1	Lower or upper senior	350-400	225	Many years	8	8
York College	120 per semester		2	2	Senior	300	180	Since 1969	10	6

Source: Colleges of the City University of New York.

44

The present UFT contract provides new teachers with a training program during their first year. However, an evaluation of this program prepared for the New York State Education Department concludes that the program had little value. One of the evaluators, Dr. James Shields, testified that the union mandates a two-hour-a-week workshop on Monday afternoons for beginning teachers. He felt that this has been a total failure. "It seems to have nothing to do with anything. I have spoken to new teachers around the city about it, and mostly they try not to go. As a matter of fact, many of them just stop going."[20] Without financial remuneration, teachers find little incentive to participate in the after-school training program.

PARAPROFESSIONALS

The only significant break in the closed personnel system has been the recruitment of paraprofessionals.

In the three demonstration districts, paraprofessionals were used extensively in the schools because they were "community people." Principals, teachers, and observers have commented on the commitment of paraprofessionals to working with ghetto children.

> Currently, some 15,000 paraprofessionals are employed in the city in a variety of job titles, mostly as educational assistants. The UFT, through its involvement in the paraprofessional program, has probably made its most significant contribution to equal employment opportunity in this aspect of the school system. Gardner Atwell, head of the Board of Education's Auxiliary Educational Career Unit, estimates that 48 percent of the paraprofessionals are black and 16 percent are Puerto Rican. Although many have been working in the schools for three years or more, less than one third are enrolled in career development programs in local colleges. The career ladder designed for paraprofessionals predicates progress on college course credits. Under current released time provisions, it will take, on the average, eight years of combined work and study to acquire a Bachelor's Degree. To date, none, except five who had prior college credits, have achieved the Associate Arts Degree, a level on the ladder providing a small pay increment, but no clear enlargement of function. No provision has been made to evaluate or accredit the years of experience and the skill acquired in in-school work except where college programs accord experience some weight in counting total credits.[21]

Clearly, the paraprofessionals are a prime source from which to enrich the teaching profession with increased minority personnel of demonstrated aptitude for teaching as a vocation. Yet traditional credentialing procedures make achievement of professional status difficult for paraprofessionals.

PROCEDURE FOR EVALUATIONS

Before 1972 teachers and supervisors generally underwent a three-year probationary period. Recently the period has been extended to five years (no tenure is being granted to new supervisors). At the end of this period, tenure is granted to satisfactory candidates. This process has been sharply attacked by educators, local boards, super-intendents, principals, and officials of the Board of Education because tenure is routinely granted. Year after year, less than a dozen teachers, and generally few administrators, are refused tenure.

As the Commission on Human Rights reported, "Some witnesses [at the commission hearings] attributed the routineness of the process to the impact of the Board of Examiners. According to them, the examination has assumed such awesome proportions in the system that once a candidate passes it there is a strong presumption that he has met the major qualifications for a permanent position in the school system."[22]

THE EXAMINATION SYSTEM

Since the early 1950s, the rating of all teacher and supervisor candidates by the Board of Examiners has been a point of controversy. The practice has been both defended as the only practical defense against political influence or favoritism in professional appointments and attacked as irrelevant to competent on-the-job performance and conducive to "inbreeding" of the staff. David Rogers has suggested one reason for this closed system: "If there is a New York City education establishment, it includes top administrators and faculty in the city colleges as well as board professionals. The links between the two are often quite close, with city college people serving on examining boards in the schools."[23]

Minor adjustments in teacher recruitment and assignment were made in the decentralization act for those schools that ranked in the bottom 45 percent of an annual city-wide reading test. Those schools could recruit teachers directly who had passed the National Teachers Examination but did not meet city requirements. They were not to be dependent on central placement. In practice this provision has not been of much use mainly because budget cuts and the union contract have forced districts to retain personnel on a seniority basis. As far as we can determine, fewer than 300 teachers have been selected on this basis.

The hiring of teachers, from the lists or those who have passed the National Teachers tests, is done by principals. Only in one district are parents involved in the hiring of teachers. Community School Board 8 has ordered that each school's PA be involved with the selection of teachers in Title I schools. The parents interview the teachers and make recommendations to the principal. This is the only district to involve parents formally in the selection of teachers.

Most CSB's have granted tenure to teachers uniformly. Under state law, anybody who has been satisfactorily employed as a regularly appointed teacher for five years receives permanent appointment. Also under state law, credit of up to three years toward permanent status may be given for satisfactory substitute service, so that, where a teacher has been satisfactorily employed as a substitute for two years, only one year of regular experience is necessary. CSB 29 took the five-year requirement to court and received an approval to grant tenure to teachers after one year. Only Districts 4, 8, 9, 13, 17, 24, and 26 have made any adjustments in the granting of tenure. Although all the boards still grant permanent status routinely, Districts 3 and 8 allow parental observation of teachers in class, and 4, 9, 13, 17, 24, and 26 publish the names of probationary instructors. In the other boards, 75 percent of them, there has been no change in the procedure of granting tenure.

Principals generally evaluate the services of all staff members, be they substitutes, probationers, or tenured personnel, since all are rated annually. These annual ratings are submitted to the district superintendent. If a teacher does not receive an "Unsatisfactory" rating, he can expect to be granted permanent appointment automatically. The district superintendent recommends permanent tenure; the CSB grants it. A few teachers have been suspended—but very few. In District 14, for instance, three teachers were denied tenure, pending the investigation of charges against them. District 4 refused tenure to two probationary teachers. The district also discontinued the service of another probationary teacher because of excessive lateness. According to the Bureau of Teacher Record, this teacher was late 86 times in one school year, 1969-70. Such instances of action by the CSB's, however, are infrequent.

Why has this situation developed? An excerpt from District 15's minutes is explanatory:

The Community School Board has run into a problem in the granting of tenure, which should never have occurred.

> We are governed by rules, contracts, laws, regulations.
> When we proceeded to investigate tenure in the district,
> we requested the names of people coming up for tenure.
> We were given twenty-five names. We sent letters to
> principals asking for reports and opinions on these
> teachers. Last week, we were given a new list, con-
> taining seventy-five names. Rating should be submitted
> sixty days before tenure date. . . . Mr. Kaplan stated that
> as President of the Community School Board, he would
> accept responsibility for the acts of others. He further
> said that "HE HAD BEEN HAD" by the system. He had
> not been forewarned by principals (who had an obligation
> to send this information in advance) and feels that unfair
> advantage was taken by the administrators.[24]

Although this CSB and others faced with such situations have learned
from them, there are limits to their power.

District 14's CSB, for example, granted tenure to a number
of teachers who served a probationary period of one and one-half
years and supervisors who had served a probationary period of one
year. The CSB was sued, and the court decided that the board did
not have power to reduce the probationary period.

A few CSB's, however, have attempted to be as independent of
central constraints as possible. CSB 4 has taken legal action challenging the constitutionality of the UFT contract's excessing-rules
provision with regard to teachers, because those excessing rules
result in de facto discrimination among the teaching staff. The CSB
offered the following explanation: "The implementation of the excessing rules of the UFT contract, in the light of the recent budget
cut, will certainly result in the loss of a significant number of minority group persons employed in teaching positions."[25]

There were, even before the cutting of staff, few blacks and
Puerto Ricans employed as teachers in the district. If teachers are
fired on the basis of "last hired, first fired"—which the excessing
rules require—then it is conceivable that a district with mostly
minority children could wind up with close to no minority personnel.

Most districts have been faced with teacher layoffs due to the
budget cuts. The problem is urgent because the extent of the cuts
are not made known immediately. Thus the local districts cannot
even decide whom to keep. Many teachers are left not knowing
whether they have a position.

District 9, in the Bronx, has taken the initiative with respect
to special personnel. Guidance counselors were assigned to the
district without the knowledge of the community school board. Board
members complained because none of the counselors could communicate

in Spanish. Of the children in the district, 43 percent are Puerto
Rican and another 4 percent are of other Spanish-speaking heritages.
Said one CSB member, "A large number of the parents of our children
cannot communicate in the English language and many of the children
in our district do not speak English. How can a counselor advise or
give guidance to children and parents when he cannot understand them
or they the counselor?"

A similar situation has been developing in District 8. At the
public meeting of July 14, 1972, it was brought to the attention of all
present that two guidance teachers were assigned to the district.
The consensus of those present was that they were not needed. The
CSB, after listening to the community, indicated that it would take
steps to have them removed.

There is also the alternate method of hiring.

> Based on the city-wide reading tests, 320 schools, mostly
> in black and Puerto Rican communities, are eligible [to
> hire under the alternate method]: [This figure includes]
> twenty-four schools in Ocean Hill-Brownsville, twenty-
> three in Bedford-Stuyvesant, twenty-seven in Central
> Harlem, four in East Harlem, nine in the Bronx, and
> several on the Upper West Side of Manhattan. Oliver
> Gibson, special assistant to the Community Superinten-
> dent in District 12, South Bronx, explains: "Barring any
> hanky-panky from the United Federation of Teachers, at
> least 120 teachers will be hired in the Fall." The UFT,
> which supports the Board of Examiners, is not enthusi-
> astic.[26]

The minor adjustments in the selection of teachers would
suggest that decentralization has not fostered any meaningful changes
in staffing arrangements. Community school boards are constrained
by legal and contract requirements that they must continue to live
with. In 1972, selected members of community boards will be represented in contract negotiations, but it is unlikely that any major
changes will be made in those contract provisions that inhibit their
actions.

Without an extensive survey of teacher's attitudes, it is difficult
to pinpoint dramatic reactions to the decentralization. Clearly for
some, particularly blacks and Puerto Ricans, access to jobs has
increased; for others, choices are more limited. With such additional
factors as budget cuts and an oversupply of candidates, it is not easy
to show that any changes are solely attributable to the decentralization.

Individual board members and principals have indicated greater
willingness by teachers to become involved in new programs, in some

cases stretching the constraints of the contract regarding work arrangements. The UFT is apparently reluctant to bring action in cases
where the teachers themselves are anxious to partake in such programs. College responses in working with local school boards and
revamping teacher training in the field are likely to add to these
activities. It does seem that responding more immediately to a local
board and parents rather than to a remote headquarters encourages
more of an orientation to client needs and interests. For some, however, this new pressure is unacceptable.

Generally, it can be said that even the minimal changes in personnel policy and procedures under community school boards should
have a cumulative effect over a period of from 5 to 10 years. We
can anticipate more emphasis on accountability for supervisors,
changes in credentialing, increased screening of teachers, and more
preservice and in-service training of teachers in the local districts.
Ultimately more responsive education programs may be an output,
but, without a greater stimulant, it is unlikely that the process can
work fast enough to show results.

Budgeting policy can be a major instrument for developing continuous evaluation of and innovation within a system, or it can be a routine bookkeeping operation supporting the status quo. The implications of budget policy are so enormous that they reflect on all aspects of educational policy.

In 1962, the New York City Board of Education was given extensive control over its budget. The Central Board exercised this control by means of a lump-sum appropriation and the ability to shift funds from one program to another without critical review. This greater flexibility did not result in increased innovation, nor did it help to encourage accountability in programming. Since 1967, the city's Bureau of the Budget has reviewed transfers, but that seems to have had little effect on the process.

Since the early 1960s, each succeeding new central board has committed itself to a more reasonable and useful budget system. A variety of experts have been called in to assist in the effort, yet recent budget issues indicate that solutions have been hard to come by. The Board has not been able to secure the necessary budget information from its own staff to use the budget as a means of determining policy. Budgeting remains a dark area of routinized operations. Budgeting is largely incremental and nonprogrammatic, with mandated expenses, such as salaries, accounting for 70 percent of the total.

The Interim Board of Education, which was appointed after passage of the Decentralization Law in 1969, continues to be plagued with the ineffectiveness of the budget process and has demonstrated its lack of control of the operation. Although it was responsible for developing new procedures under decentralization, the effort made was to begin to prepare an allocation formula, which it has not yet completed. Local boards have not made significant inputs into the budget process and function largely as bookkeeping agencies. Certainly community and parent groups have even less influence on the determination of the budget and allocation of resources.

THE COMMUNITY BOARDS AND THE BUDGET

Many observers of the public schools maintain that in order for a group to have significant power in any area of the education program it must have control over both the expense and capital budgets. Nearly all CSB members interviewed identified budgeting as one of the most important issues with which they must deal, yet they indicated that they have not been very effective in this area.

The amount of funds allocated to the community school districts is dependent on the total education budget for the city and the structure for dividing the total between the city and community boards. Both the budgets for 1970-71 and 1971-72 were submitted by the city Board in similar form. The separation of CSB monies from city Board monies has proven impossible to achieve under present budget structure.

Expense Budget

The Decentralization Law states that the CSB's must hold public hearings and submit budget estimates for their activities to the chancellor. These estimates may be modified by the chancellor after consultation with the community superintendents. They are then submitted by him—along with an estimate for central Board activities— to the Board of Estimate and the City Council.

Upon approval of these bodies, the chancellor advocates the monies to the CSB's on the basis of "objective formulas" arrived at each year by the central Board after consultation with the chancellor, the CSB's and the mayor. The chancellor is also authorized to make special allocations from appropriate city Board funds to individual CSB's for special needs or innovative programs. These objective formulas were never completed.

The law also states that the chancellor will develop procedures so that CSB's can establish and modify annual schedules for the expenditure of appropriated funds. These procedures were, " to the maximum extent feasible," to enable the CSB's to do this without prior approval, "subject to regulations which the Chancellor or budget director will establish to assure . . . compliance with the legal and fiscal requirements."[1] Although these procedures were to have been established relatively promptly, they have not yet been developed.

Most of the expense budget consists of instructional cost; an Institute for Community Studies report of the budget process in 1969 placed the estimate at 70 percent.2 Because the CSB's are bound by the UFT's contract with the city Board, local discretion is drastically curtailed.

At present, the CSB's are allowed three official representatives who sit in on the contract negotiations, but they are far outnumbered by the other groups, and their impact will most probably be insignificant.

The vast amount of mandatory expenditures for teachers' salaries plus established ratios for specialized personnel make it clear that the budgetary power of the CSB's is of a very limited nature. In this vital area, the CSB's cannot change schedules without the chancellor's approval.

Another related limit on the CSB's budgetary powers occurs when the city Board, through a budget cut or some other exigency, excesses personnel. These persons are then assigned to the respective districts or to central headquarters but must be paid from local district budgets. The result is that the CSB's are severely curtailed in their deployment of personnel and use of funds.

The central Board has the authority to transfer such employees. A section of the decentralization law reads:

> Within sixty days after February 16, 1970, the interim board, acting through the Chancellor, will transfer to each community board authority over all city district employees serving in or in connection with schools and programs under that community board's jurisdiction. All employees serving in or in connection with programs which continue under central jurisdiction will be retained. The interim board acting through the Chancellor can either transfer to appropriate community boards or retain other city district employees.3

It is clear that the central Board did have the power to transfer personnel. But sixty days after February 16, 1970 have long passed, so continuation of this practice seems legally questionable.

Some districts have sought to maintain their autonomy against the city Board's encroachments. A direct clash between community school board 21 and the central Board was avoided by the Mansfield decision, prior to which it had been unofficial city Board policy that acting assistant principals be allowed to serve for one year only. Faced with severe budget cuts, community school board 21 decided to continue some individuals in acting assistant positions past the one-year limitation in order to save money. Interviewed prior to

TABLE 8

Constraints[a] Imposed on Community School
Boards by Decentralization Law[b]

I. Expense Budget	II. Allocation of Central Funds	III. Special Funds
Budget Request	The chancellor allocates the funds to the community school boards in accordance with "objective formulas" established each year by the city Board in consultation with the mayor and the community school boards.	a. Community boards will be able to contract directly for private and public nonformula funds, which may be used for special programs, but not eliminate existing positions and employees.
a. The chancellor may modify community school boards' budget estimates after consulting with the district superintendents.		
b. The city Board must approve these modified estimates after they are incorporated into the consolidated budget.		b. Community school boards cannot apply as local educational agencies for state and federal funds distributed to the city on a formula basis (Title I and state urban education monies).
c. The city Board's budget hearings last only four days, not allowing much time for community school board input.		
d. Once the city Board has approved the consolidated budget, it will be submitted in the normal city budget process to the mayor and, following any modifications he may make, to the Board of Estimate and City Council.		c. The community school boards will be limited in the total dollar amount of its proposals for such funds by an apportionment among community school boards, according to a formula reflecting the same economic and educational factors as those that determine the chancellor's objective formula.
e. The City Council and Board of Estimate, before their approval is granted, must hold public hearings, which last only about a week. Again, local input is severely curtailed.		

54

IV. Capital Budget

a. City Board is responsible for submitting a capital budget to the City Planning Commission. The budget must be approved by the mayor, the Board of Estimate, and the City Council.

b. Community school boards can submit proposals for schools to the chancellor, mayor, Board of Estimate, City Council, and Planning Commission.

c. The city Board retains responsibility and control over capital constructions subject to the duties and authority of other city agencies.

d. The community school boards can select proposed sites for submission to the city site-selection board.

e. The city Board retains responsibility for the care, custody, and control of school property.

f. A community school board cannot spend more than $250,000 for repairs in a fiscal year without special authorization from the chancellor.

[a]State constraints: "Funds may not be shifted from the capital to the expense budget or vice versa unless there is an offsetting shift in the other direction" (Marcia Marker Feld, A Basic Guide to the New York City School Budget Process [New York: Institute for Community Studies, 1969], p. 15).

City constraints: "There is serious doubt as to whether the city charter provisions apply to the city board and to the Community School Boards absent, a specific provision of State Law. The State Constitution declares public education to be a State function. . . . The city board and the Community School Boards are created independently of the city by mandate of State Law" (Ibid, p. 16).

[b]The community school boards are also bound by the city boards with the UFT, CSA, Custodians' Union, and other groups.

55

the Mansfield decision, one member of community school board 21 felt that some action against this central policy would be necessary.

Certain districts are disturbed about the monetary problems that follow from the busing of disadvantaged children into their schools. For example, CSB 24 was promised last year that all disadvantaged children coming into the district would be accompanied by Title I and state urban money. The city Board did send $100 of the $269 Title I funds per child, but the other $169 from federal monies was never received. As Joseph Whalen, a CSB member stated, "With the inadequate funds given to us for these children, we are unable to provide the extra help that is needed. In addition, the learning process for our own children is slowed down."[4] CSB 24 advised the city Board that it "will not accept any open-enrollment students in District 24 next term unless the full allocation of their Title I and State-Urban funds are given to District 24."[5] District 7 children being bused into the schools of District 11 were only granted $80 in District 11 instead of the $120 they would receive as Title I children in District 7.

Other predominantly middle-class districts share these worries. CSB 22, for example, has acknowledged an obligation to receive open-enrollment children but believes that its first obligation is to its own children. This district, however, has been more successful in getting the state and federal monies in question, receiving about 70 percent of the full amount for each child.

Included in the expense budget are the operation and maintenance of plant. The law provides that the general responsibility for the care and control of school property will remain with the city Board. The city Board will hire all school custodians. This can have the same unfortunate effect on the employment of minority groups as the city Board's handling of all construction contracts. Some have argued that the custodians' union supported the UFT in the Ocean Hill-Brownsville confrontation because it feared that community control of schools would remove white workers in the custodial services. For the past year District 10 has been fighting with the central Board over control of the custodial contract. District 10 recognized the power of the custodial union and is attempting to gain its loyalty.

District 8, when it had to hire guards to police its schools, sent out bids to the various policing agencies with the stipulation that people hired had to live in the district and that the contracting agency would train them if need be. The Burns Agency accepted the contract.

Over 51 percent of the 79 board members interviewed felt they should receive remuneration for personal expenses. Board members in districts 4, 21, and 24 stated that the failure to cover board members'

expenses impeded many individuals from serving on the boards.
Examples of remuneration were few and involved small amounts.
District 27 provides each member of the board with a telephone for
board business and reimbursement for travel expenses, including
10 cents a mile and repayment of tolls. CSB members in District 2
have been reimbursed for expenses. The largest amount was $400.
Four other members received an average amount of $100 each for
the year. District 13 reimbursed one member $50 to cover phone
costs. District 12 reimburses board members from a fund for
transportation costs.

Capital Budget

With respect to the planning and construction of capital projects,
the powers of the CSB's are severely limited. The decentralization
law charges the city Board, through the chancellor, with the responsi
bility of "submitting a capital budget for construction, remodelling and
enlargement of all school system facilities to the city planning
commission." The powers of the CSB's merely entail submitting
proposals for schools within their jurisdiction to the chancellor,
mayor, Board of Estimate, City Council, and City Planning Commission.
The city Board, through the chancellor, "will continue to employ all
personnel required for construction and design." However, the law
does give the CSB's certain advisory powers in the areas of "site
selection and design and construction of facilities . . . under their
jurisdiction."[6] For example, the CSB's may select proposed sites
for submission to the city site-selection board, select architects
for particular projects from among several on the panel proposed
by the city Board, and the like.

The limited power of the CSB's in this area has in some cases
resulted in considerable delays and interference with discretion in
local educational policy-making. District 15, for example, experienced considerable difficulty in obtaining the approval of the
Division of School Planning and Research for two mini-schools. The
central agency refused to give the go-ahead on these projects—which
the CSB and community believed were desperately needed—because
the plans did not meet certain space requirements. After several
months of bickering with the planning division, the CSB did get
permission to proceed—and funds were released—with plans that
differed only in minor ways from those initially submitted. But the
limited power of the CSB and the lack of responsiveness of the central
bureaucracy meant that many children were deprived of a mini-school
experience.

Another and similar situation developed in District 26 over the modernization of PS 159. The job began, but the CSB later wanted to change the central bureaucracy's specifications for the rest of the job, which cost $20,000. The project was halted because of the central Board's veto, the delay cost being over $16,000 a month. Because of the hassle, the job was not done for eight months; thus the delay cost was significantly greater than the cost of the protested section.

Despite bureaucratic inefficiency, some districts have proceeded quite well with their construction projects. District 18 has followed the central guidelines and has been able to open several annexes to schools, which have helped ease the overcrowding of the schools. These annexes, according to one member of the CSB, could not have opened within the previously structured system. District 22 has also proceeded quite well in the construction of IS 387. The selection of a reuse design for this school is supposed to save some six months to a year in completing the project.

Although the CSB's have little or no legal power in this area, it is perhaps fair to say that they can exercise some informal power. One can conclude, however, little more than that some CSB's have this power in spite of the decentralization law.

As was noted earlier, the city Board retains the responsibility to employ all personnel required for construction and design. Part of the motivation behind this perhaps exists in the Board of Education's plan to force the construction trade unions to admit minority-group members by withholding construction contracts. According to the Board's resolution of February 18, 1970, an acceptable plan for on-the-job training programs involving as many workers from disadvantaged areas as is practical is required by contractors and subcontractors on all new school construction and major modernization contracts. Mayor John Lindsay, furthermore, signed an executive order effective September 1, 1970 that required contractors working on city construction projects, or projects assisted by the city, to hire one minority trainee for every four journeymen on the job.

This means that projects already approved by the Board of Estimate have very often not been constructed. For example, in District 29, two projects are involved: a mini-school for PS 34 in Queens Village and a wing for IS 231 in Springfield Gardens. The president of the CSB has demanded an end to what he branded the city Board's "starve-into-submission-certain-unions" policy. His district has not had construction starts since the present city Board assumed office in 1970. Meanwhile, he states, continuing inflation is increasing the cost of the projects so that existing appropriations are becoming "increasingly inadequate." Furthermore, the insufficiency of seats for District 29's children has resulted in involved

legal disputes with adjacent districts in which the excess children
have to be placed.

The CSB in District 3 has urged, on the other hand, that the
city Board and contractors see to it that minority-group members
are not discriminated against in the construction of the Martin Luther
King High School. The contract in question between the Caristo Construction Company and the Board of Education apparently violates
both the Board's and mayor's commitment to on-the-job training
programs on city construction programs. This leads one to conclude
that whatever the city Board's intent, it has failed to push through
implementation of its own resolution, even where the community
demands it.

Another such incident occurred in District 6. When PS 187
was to have its kitchen modernized, the CSB president and the community superintendent were ordered to utilize an engineering firm
selected by the Office of School Buildings. This did not allow a
board that has actively sought out qualified minority-group workers
to attempt to bring in an engineering firm of its own choice. In effect,
this CSB felt that it was denied the responsibility of fixing its own
kitchens. The CSB complied with the directive and in effect did not
exert its rights.

The above indicates that there is little rationale for retaining
central control over construction because contractors can be forced
to hire minority personnel; in fact, it would seem from the evidence
that local boards would be more likely to fulfill that goal. Although
it is reasonable, from certain perspectives, that construction should
be handled centrally, there are very real advantages in giving the
CSB's a greater discretion in this area as well. Delays in construction
could be minimized (as in District 29), and particular local needs met
(as in District 6).

As we have indicated, the CSB's have advisory powers in the
area of site selection. This is not to say that the CSB's play much
of a part in decisions to build new schools. For example, in District
14 (as, perhaps, in several others), everyone recognized the need for
a new school but had little to do in bringing it about; as one CSB
member stated, "110 [the Board's headquarters is at 110 Livingston
Street] decided to give us a school." Although there is usually agreement about the need for schools, this consensus diminishes when
the site must be selected. As one CSB member put it, "Everyone
wants another school, but no one wants it on his block."

The site-selection process brings the CSB into contact with
several groups—homeowners, businesses, other school districts,
etc. The protest of the sixty-odd homeowners in District 24 in Queens
was much in the news in 1971. In District 15, a large business concern, which would provide many jobs for the community, is being

constructed on one of the proposed sites for a new school. An inter-
district dispute broke out between District 22 and District 18 when
the latter feared that having the former's school built close to its
boundary would lead to turmoil within its own district. These are
the kinds of concerns with which the various CSB's must deal in the
site-selection process.

As in the past, it seems that the CSB's act as a buffer between
the central Board and the community, although they have little power.

Before the CSB begins its site-selection proceedings, the general
vicinity of the new school has already been designated in the adopted
capital budget. As we have suggested, the CSB site hearings provide
various community groups with an input into the process of delineating
the more specific neighborhood of the school. These proceedings
can be significant insofar as affected groups can be heard and a
proposed site arrived at.

Yet the formal power with regard to site selection resides with
the Site Selection Board, which must approve all proposed sites of
the CSB. The mayor, City Council, City Planning Commission, and
other city agencies are also involved in the process.

Their intervention has, in some cases, stringently limited even
the advisory powers that the CSB's do have. District 24 was mentioned
earlier with regard to the much publicized controversy concerning
the proposed school site, which would have displaced some sixty-odd
homeowners. It was in favor of the site, yet action on the sorely
needed high school was delayed for a considerable period of time
because the board did not and does not have the authority to act de-
cisively in the matter.

The situation in District 8 provides another example of the
CSB's limited power in the site-selection process. The City Planning
Commission had apparently decided on a site for PS 182X without
consulting that district's CSB. The CSB then took a show-cause order
against the commission and also urged the community to begin a
letter-writing campaign to both the Mayor and the Bronx Borough
President. However, the court ruling was not favorable to the CSB.
The district, because of lack of funds, has decided not to appeal the
decision. Once again a CSB may become unpopular in the eyes of
some community members who believe the board should have exercised
the power it in fact did not have.

Perhaps the most that can be said for the site-selection procedure prescribed by the decentralization law is that it permits more
local inputs than the previous procedure. But, since the CSB's have
little actual power, frustrations arise both for the boards and the
communities.

When the board of District 2 tried to operate its own lunch and
breakfast programs, it found that it was budgeted to handle 9,000

children at a cost of 40 cents each. The board soon discovered that
it could serve the same children on the local level at the low cost of
from 20 to 28 cents. This eventually amounted to a saving of $37,000,
which was returned to the Bureau of Lunches. District 2 also made
significant progress in the renovation of school kitchens, equiping
eight schools in four weeks to serve frozen foods, at an average cost
of $3,000 per school. The central Board's program called for the
renovation of some 400 outmoded kitchens throughout the city at the
rate of six to ten per year at a cost of $100,000 to $250,000 each.
District 3 has also achieved some gains in this area by converting
kitchens to serve fresh foods.

 This does show what the CSB's can do when they take the initiative. Other districts such as 10 and 12 are following the lead of
District 2.

 Largely because of faulty enrollment estimates by the CSB's
for the 1971-72 school year, the Board of Education had to reallocate
$4.6 million in authorized operating funds among the districts. Under
the reallocation, 11 of the 31 local districts lost amounts ranging
from $55,555 to $1,045,486, which went to other districts with the
individual amounts ranging from $697 to $621,759. This reallocation
did not involve the question of whether the school system had exceeded
the operating budget granted by the city. The total budget allocation
was not to be affected by the problem, only the amounts allotted to
individual districts (see Table 9).

Conclusion

 Budget allocation by formula as required by the decentralization
law is a significant reform, but it does not necessarily give any new
budgetary power to community school boards. The Board of Education
commissioned McKinsey and Company, a management-consultant
firm, to conduct a pilot study of the management capabilities of a
sample district, 14. The report, issued in January 1971, indicated
that "the budget process now serves little purpose at the district
level." Two main reasons were posited:

> First, various budgetary and legal requirements—outside
> the control of the [district] superintendent—require a high
> proportion of the district's available funds: most tax-levy
> funds are used to pay teachers, and allocations for this
> purpose are determined primarily by centrally negotiated
> UFT contract restrictions on maximum class size and
> preparation periods.
> Second, . . . the superintendent's actual financial
> control is even further limited by the actions of other

TABLE 9

School Board Allocations, 1971-72
(in dollars)

District	District Entitled to:	Owned by District (-) or Due District (+)	
Manhattan			
1 Lower East Side	15,784,732	+	20,432
2 Lower West Side-East Midtown	19,338,797	-	86,914
3 Lower and Upper Park West	18,060,247	-	136,355
4 East Harlem	17,197,223	-	540,334
5 Central Harlem	19,709,569	+	116,514
6 Inwood-Washington Heights	16,472,290	+	679
Bronx			
7 South Bronx	24,837,978	+	98,288
8 Clason Point-Throgs Neck	27,813,501	-	55,555
9 Concourse	29,071,289	+	621,759
10 Fordham-Riverdale	23,866,301	+	243,436
11 Williamsbridge-North Bronx	23,164,624	-	826,766
12 Morrisania	27,618,523	-	522,893
Brooklyn			
13 Brooklyn Heights-Bedford Stuyvesant	19,979,772	-	269,370
14 Williamsburg-Greenpoint	24,185,231	+	69,593
15 South Brooklyn-Park Slope	21,880,897	+	282,123
16 Bushwick-Ridgewood	29,030,095	-	479,803
17 Crown Heights-Flatbush	20,971,709	+	325,817
18 Canarsie-East Flatbush	17,794,016	-	391,662
19 East New York	30,794,818	-	296,688
20 Bay Ridge-Bensonhurst	22,415,251	+	230,332
21 Gravesend-Coney Island	23,417,803	+	108,067
22 Midwood-Sheepshead Bay	23,405,306	+	185,033
23 Brownsville	18,780,423	-	1,045,486
Queens			
24 Maspeth-Middle Village	19,256,869	+	348,882
25 Flushing-College Point	22,250,158	+	131,630
26 Bayside-Douglaston	17,755,960	+	426,964
27 Richmond Hill-South Rockaway	23,983,959	+	250,630
28 Forest Hills-Jamaica	23,321,522	+	171,594
29 Queens Village-Springfield Gardens	20,966,039	+	43,921
30 Astoria-Woodside	19,510,163	+	498,144
Richmond			
31 Entire borough	29,256,522	+	477,997

Source: The New York Times, March 8, 1972.

groups in the system. In fact, many key decisions—e.g.,
the ultimate utilization of teachers—are made at other
levels.[7]

Several community school boards have refused to abide by budget
cuts and have challenged unsuccessfully the validity of the entire
budget process. District 7 refused to accept the cuts. The central
Board sent a planned budget to District 7's office, which the district
eventually was forced to accept. District 3 instituted a law suit over
the mandated budget cuts and lost the case. These actions indicate
the overwhelming power of the central Board in budget matters.

The provisions of the new allocation system call for each community school district to receive allocations according to modules.
In 1970-71 boards could transfer only small amounts (and only from
the administrative module) to other modules. Thus the major pro-
portion of funds remains out of the control of local boards.

Community school boards will not be able to discharge their
responsibility for management until the central Board identifies,
separates, and allocates all funds for these boards and provides the
kind of technical information to the boards so that they can engage
in the budget process.

In general, the CSB's have not accomplished much in the area
of budget management. Anything they have done has been in rather
insignificant matters. CSB 22 for example, was able to agree that
"the sum of $5,947 be reallocated from personnel service for Con-
tinuing Education to materials and supplies for Continuing Education."[8]
A similar shift of funds enabled the CSB to keep the evening community
center program running a bit longer. District 2 did save $37,000
on its school lunches and was able to equip eight school kitchens at an
average cost of $3,000 per school. This was in sharp contrast to the
central Board's renovation of kitchens at a cost of $100,000 to
$250,000. But the case of District 2 seems to be the exception rather
than the rule.

The major reason for CSB ineffectiveness, as we have suggested,
is the lack of any significant power. The constraints of the UFT and
other union contracts and the city Board's delaying tactics in restructuring the budget increase the CSB's problems in exercising control
over their operating and capital budgets.

Another reason for the lack of activity in budgeting affairs is
that the subject is so complex that it eludes the grasp of even the
most adroit board members. Of those interviewed, even lawyers and
actuaries—who by profession are probably most equipped to understand such matters—suspect that grasping just the fundamentals of
the budgeting process would require their full-time attention.

Several of the districts have considerably enlarged their district office staffs. All districts have or are in the process of hiring a business manager at the starting salary of between $17,000 and $18,500. This has given many districts the needed expertise in finance. The following districts have a business manager, or are searching for one: 1, 3, 4, 5, 6, 7, 8, 9, 10, 11, 12, 13, 16, 18, 21, 22, 24, 25, 26, 27, 28, 29, and 30. Districts without business managers are 17, 19, and 23. In the various districts, the staffs of the community superintendent and the community school board range from about 25 to 45. The district office budget could vary from sector to sector depending on the size of staff. Some CSB's have an executive assistant responsible directly to the board. This is a noncompetitive civil service position that can serve the board in discharging its administrative duties. The hope is that the executive assistant would free the CSB of many of its more routine tasks so that it could direct its energies to some of the more basic issues involved in the education of children. Such a position would presumably enable the CSB's to grapple with budgetary matters in a more skillful fashion. By early 1972, no more than five CSB's had executive assistants.

There has been some controversy over the matter of public aid to parochial schools. The Board of Education has not officially dealt with this issue. Some CSB's have supported public financial assistance for parochial schools. (See the discussion of the role of parochial groups in Chapter 1.)

There is little evidence to indicate that PTA's, community action groups, and other organizations have been significantly involved by the CSB's in many of the budgetary proceedings. This has been true even in those districts that tend to give the community a real role in other matters. In part, this is because the CSB's view their communities as passive entities to be consulted and "present" at public meetings, but excluded at the point of decision. Participation in the budgetary process is further complicated by the fact of timing, the budget allocations are simply not known until late spring or early summer when it is most difficult for parent and community groups to have the impact they might otherwise aim for. Several CSB's have been the target of strong community criticism for their failures to seek more money from the city Board for the community districts.

THE TITLE I SECTION OF BUDGET

One salient fact has emerged in the handling of Title I funds for programs: the importance of professional control. "Since 1965, virtually all state and federal funds for compensatory education granted to the City were spent in programs spelled out or controlled by the

provisions of the UFT Contract," concluded Anthony Cresswell and
Paul Irvin in their study of Title I.[9] Moreover, that pattern emerged
prior to the passage of the Elementary and Secondary Education Act
of 1965. To a large extent it still exists today.

Programs such as the More Effective Schools (MES), Strengthened
Early Childhood (SEC), Five Primary Schools (5P), and Experimental
Elementary programs were either directly mandated by the UFT
contract or based on a clause calling for smaller classes and increased
use of specialized personnel. The first four programs accounted for
$48.4 million of the $75 million budgeted for the community school
boards in 1970-71.

The total allocated to New York City for 1970-71 was $110
million with $66.5 million budgeted for the community boards. When
aid to nonpublic schools and district open enrollment allocations are
subtracted from the money given to the community boards, $16.25
million remained for the local school districts. Only the direction of
14.5 percent of the original allocation to New York City was actually
decided by the community school boards. This figure was 3 percent
less than the total dollar expenditure for programs directed by the
central Board, and only 3.4 percent greater than the Title I funds
devoted to contingency operations.

The rationale for the UFT sponsorship of various Title I programs should be evident. These programs are primarily quantitative,
dealing with reduction of class size and increases in teaching and
specialized personnel. They make classroom work easier and create
more jobs.

Although the Board of Education has been continuously pressured
to increase local control over Title I funds, it was not until June, 1970
that any innovations were implemented. Beginning with money spent
for the 1970-71 academic year, only two-thirds of the Title I money
would continue to be budgeted through the local boards to MES, SEC,
and Primary School Projects. The remaining one-third of the Title I
money would be released to the individual boards, to be used at the
discretion of the community board. (The plan was to turn control
over to the community boards by thirds over a three-year period.)
That first year the community board was forced to choose between
funding the mandated programs completely or contradicting the spirit
of a union contract to which it had no real substantive input. To be
sure, not all districts reacted in the same manner. But more important than any individual area's action, the change by the Board of
Education prepared the way for further decentralization of control
over Title I funds.

One year after the decision to give community boards control
over one-third of the mandated programs' dollars, the New York
state supreme court ruled for community school boards in a case

brought by Community School Board 3. Citing the decentralization
law, the court ruled "that the most reasonable interpretation of Section
2590-1-14 (d) [section of decentralization law dealing with federal
funds] is that Community School Board 3 has been given power by the
State Legislature to determine the use of Title One funds without
review. . . ." In effect, the court ruled that the Board of Education
could not contract away funds designated to local boards. Only the
community school boards could decide the allocation of the money.
This historic decision was declared a victory for community control.
Each community was now to have the financial mobility to create "a
community-oriented approach" to education. In addition to this judicial
decree, Chancellor Harvey Scribner reinforced a federal decree that
all Title I advisory committees were to be composed of at least 51
percent parents and that at most 49 percent of the committees could
be school personnel. In 1972, community school boards had fought
for control of Title I dollars. The courts had not only enforced
their rights but the parents, fighting local boards for positions in
the decision-making process, were also to control 51 percent of
the advisory committees. An important skirmish in the battle for
control of budgetary management had apparently been won by the
community.

But inspection of the 31 school boards' actual operation indicates
that the court case did not bring about community control of Title I
funds. A survey of all school boards, answered by 14 district Title I
coordinators, demonstrated that, for the 1971-72 academic year,
47.5 percent of all Title I funds went for the formerly centrally mandated programs (see Table 10). District 3, which filed the suit against
central domination, still spent 67.7 percent of its funds for the SEC
and 5P programs. In response to the question "What factors were
considered in your district's decision to invest a substantial amount
of its Title I funds in SEC," the Title I coordinator in District 3
answered, "They were mandated by the Central Board of Education
despite our lawsuit." Even when a community wants to change, the
Board of Education can delay innovation. Cresswell and Irvin show
that the central Board can prevail through delays in approving programs and dispersing funds.[10]

Central control over the distribution of Title I funds has caused
considerable problems in Districts 18, 20, 22, 24, 25, and 26. Under
the decentralization law, the Board of Education can change the allocation formula within the limits set by state and federal guidelines.
Section 2590-i 11d of the law gives the chancellor the power to appropriate funds to local boards

> provided, however, that in the case of such special funds
> community boards shall not be considered local educational

TABLE 10

Use of Title I Funds for MES, SEC, and
5P Programs, 1971-72[a]
(in dollars)

District	(1) Funds Received	(2) Money Spent on SEC	MES	5P	Percent Column 2 of Column 1
1	3,075,802	1,024,213	1,226,532	—	72.3
3	3,095,280	1,833,724	—	287,568	65.2
7	5,218,524	2,400,149	—	238,417	50.6
9	5,635,764	1,673,443	472,871	—	38.1
12	5,700,000	1,647,644	—	—	28.9
14	5,032,118	1,656,374	400,794	—	42.8
15	3,701,020	1,451,630	910,000	—	64.4
20	1,750,047	235,837	—	—	13.5
24	479,086	285,203	—	—	66.5
29	1,570,879	186,609	327,403	—	32.5
30	972,266	366,400	—	—	37.7
Totals	37,194,797	12,761,226	3,337,600	525,485	44.7

[a]That is, after CSB 3's lawsuit.

Source: Returned questionnaires sent originally to all district Title I coordinators.

    agencies; and provided further that the total amount of
    such proposals submitted by any community board shall
    not exceed the amount of an appointment made by the
    chancellor on the basis of a formula determined by the
    city board . . .

This power to change the allocation has cost at least one district
(25) over $500,000 in federal funds since 1970. With the strict state
and city guidelines requiring that Title I funds be given to those districts and schools whose populations are 38 percent poverty children,
districts with only pockets of poor children receive no money for
special services—except for open enrollment children. This has
forced districts 18, 20, 22, 24, 25, and 26, which will lose all Title I
funds, to consider court action to save their programs.

The amounts of Title I dollars for eligible districts are considerably different in 1972-73 from the preceding year. District 27, de-
scribing itself as "considerably distraught," requested a special
meeting with the director of Funded Programs at the central Board
to review the formula. The CSB felt that either the poverty "figures
and their meaning have been misinterpreted or considerations of
some of the special poverty conditions have been obscured."11

Districts that involve parents in the decision-making process
may be expected to allocate funds to different programs should projects
fail to meet expectations. A further continuation of the Strengthening
Early Childhood program in District 3 would mean that the program
is meeting the parents' expectations. But the inclusion of parents to
the same extent as District 3 has been the exception not the rule. To
date, only Districts 3, 7, 8, 13, and 17 have tried to make parent participation meaningful (see Table 11). In these districts, the advisory
committees have some substantive input that can shape and affect any
Title I programs and policies. The other districts seem to feel com-
fortable operating in a manner strikingly similar to the patterns
usually attributed to 110 Livingston Street. Federal guidelines over
Title I required that all advisory committees be at least 51 percent
parents. In June 1971, at the time of Scribner's reminder to the
community school boards to create Title I advisory committees composed of a minimum of 51 percent parents, Districts 22 and 24 had
advisory committees composed of only 36 percent parents. They have
since revised their committees. Districts 1, 3, and 7 all have advisory
committees with parents making up at least 74 percent of the advisory
committees.

With Title I funds, District 6 in Manhattan has instituted a
program, "Orientation and Adjustment of the New Arrivals in the
School Community," designed to foster image-building in young students.
District 2 in Manhattan has concentrated on prekindergarten education
with federal funds used to renovate a rented facility. District 12 in
the Bronx has spent Title I money for bilingual research. Many other
districts (2, 6, 13, 23, 24, etc.) utilize summer programs that stress
reading and mathematical skills for low achievers or afternoon centers
that provide both educational and recreational activities aimed at
improving the quality of life for poverty children.

Although many boards have utilized Title I funds for effective
programs benefiting poor children, some districts have violated the
intent as well as the spirit of Title I for reasons that involve the
interests of middle-class parents and the mechanics of disbursement.
Many middle-class parents have sought federal funds for projects
that are not directed to the needs of underachievers. These include
a Science Club in District 14, a questionable program in a district
whose poverty children have scored almost two years below their

TABLE 11

Composition of Title I Advisory Committees
in Selected Districts, 1972

Dis-trict	Total	Parents	School Per-sonnel	Com-munity Mem-bers	Paro-chial Inter-ests	Students	Other	Percent Parents
1	34	20	9	4	1	a	a	73.5
3	42	23	6	5	1	4	3	83.3
7	32	22	2	4	4	a	a	73.8
11	27	14	2	11	a	a	a	51.0
12	a	a	a	a	a	a	a	50.0
13	a	a	a	a	a	a	a	51.0
14	a	a	a	a	a	a	a	51.0
15	a	a	a	a	a	a	a	51.0
17	17	17	a	a	a	a	a	100.0
20	27	18	a	a	a	a	a	66.0
24	35	a	a	a	a	a	a	51.0
26	35	20	a	a	a	a	a	57.1
30	18	13	3	1	1	a	a	69.9

aNumbers not supplied by district coordinators.

Source: Returned questionnaires originally sent to all district Title I coordinators.

classmates in reading. In addition, several districts have classes on ecology and environment and computer clubs. These projects have resulted from the pressures brought by middle-class parents seeking programs for their children. Proposals that on paper appear to benefit the slow learners, in practice, by-pass them.

Under the influence of community boards, the paraprofessional program has begun to gain support. Each district has found a need for remedial classes in reading and mathematics in early grades and hired individuals who, although not licensed teachers, could have the expertise to help with the classes. The paraprofessional lines have enabled districts to involve more bilingual people in the edu-cational process.

CONCLUSION

If effective decentralization is to be implemented, a decentralized budgeting procedure under the district boards should be developed and implemented. (CSB's have been working to achieve this.) Such a process should establish reliable performance and cost analysis on an individual school basis. The budget could then be used as a management and policy tool for rewarding workable programs and eliminating costly and unproductive projects.

Full state assumptions* of financial responsibility for education would encourage the implementation of district budgeting assuming each of the districts were identified as independent recipients of state aid. District collective bargaining supplemental to state agreements would reduce the excessive constraints which so greatly limit budgeting as a policy process.

---

*The California case should raise the issue of financial reform of education as a more immediate concern.

CENTRAL BOARD POLICY UNDER
DECENTRALIZATION

Educational policy in the New York City school system poses a paradoxical problem for serious educational analysts. On the one hand, there can be no doubt that the nation's greatest educational variety can be found, and nearly every educational approach and curriculum finally gets tried, in the school system. On the other hand, there can also be little doubt that the New York City schools are failing their clients, particularly the urban poor.

Fully one-third of New York City public school pupils are one or more years behind in reading compared with national norms, and the latest tests show that number edging toward 40 percent. Only one-third of New York high school students go on to college, compared to nearly half for the nation as a whole. The dropout rate of black and Puerto Rican students is over 50 percent. Approximately 14,000 pupils were suspended in 1971.

These figures on achievement are corroborated by other statistics on teacher and pupil absences indicating the serious malaise of the school system. Of all major cities New York has the lowest pupil attendance (83 percent in 1971-72 and steadily dropping). In 1930-31, the attendance rate was 92.3 percent, and in 1965-66 it was 87 percent. One school, Boys High, had a 51 percent figure of attendance. And a recent Board of Education study reported teacher absenteeism as having increased by 50 percent in the school years 1966-67, 1967-68, and 1968-69.[1]

Yet New York City is renowned for the scope of diverse educational programs instituted in its various schools. In the last few years, it has followed a progressive educational policy concerning

71

both curriculum and pupils. One can visit an open integrated class-
room, a Montessori classroom, a school without walls, Bereiter-
Engleman schools, the latest bilingual classroom, talking typewriters
and computerized education, and a school based on the MES program.
In short, nearly every new educational idea has been instituted in New
York City.

Moreover, the New York City public school system has pioneered
in adopting rules pertaining to student rights. In 1971, the city
drafted a bill of student rights attempting to improve public policy.
One seasoned educational observer credits the school system with
high marks for its far reaching ability to absorb new trends and
methods. The New York City Bureau of Curriculum, according to this
observer, is considered one of the top agencies nationally, attracting
highly qualified professionals.

The major difficulty in improving educational policy has been
implementation. Critics contend that the more enterprising educational
innovations are implemented on an experimental and piecemeal basis:
One can find exciting educational ventures in scattered classrooms,
but little effort is made to translate these successful recipes into
programs that might affect substantial numbers of students. This, in
the eyes of many critics, was the case under the old, pre-CSB system,
whereby educational policy was determined by professionals and
trickled down to a school level. The community school boards have
been unable to counter the previous trend due to lack of time and
experience and because of limits on their powers over curriculum
and pupil policy. In some schools in some districts, of course, the
boards can claim achievements of a high caliber.

The school decentralization law diffused educational policy
responsibility to the community boards. The community boards could
establish policy concerning curriculum, textbooks, and evaluation
with the approval of central headquarters (the chancellor), provided
that these programs meet standards set by the chancellor, and with
the exception of special policies adopted by the central Board affecting
all districts. In two instances, the central Board mandated a black
history program and a narcotics education program in all districts.
Few of the community boards have been able to muster significant
energy to implement innovative educational programs. District 18's
board instituted a few programs such as the Block School, which is a
variant of the open classroom for preschoolers. But some plans have
been continued year after year without ostensible signs of productivity.
For example, the MES program, initiated by the United Federation of
Teachers some seven years ago, provides saturation teacher and
special services for ghetto children. This program— hailed as an
educational panacea—has failed to live up to expectations. Preliminary
studies have not shown substantial gains in pupil achievement. With

some 17,000 pupils, the MES program is the most widely known and expensive project in the country for poor children. The latest evaluation in 1971 by the Psychological Corporation observed a program that greatly enhanced the pupil's image in terms of understanding, confidence, and learning desire but did not produce academic gains. Still the MES program continues.

Under the new community system, little has changed. The community has little voice in determining policy. Significantly, recently appointed Chancellor Harvey Scribner has made the top-priority items in his administration implementation of decentralization and an effort to change personnel policy, rather than curriculum advances. Scribner has promoted minor ventures at this time—a school without walls, an auxiliary high school, and the like—but there has been no major educational thrust so far, except for an "Innovative Center," which is too new to evaluate fully. Also, his staff is beginning a Study and Implementation program that will theoretically give the central Board of Education a blueprint for future action.

Tracking

It can be readily seen why teachers, on first reaction, would prefer homogeneous grouping of students according to ability, achievement, or other criteria. Teaching "tracked" pupils requires less effort. Perhaps that is why the United Federation of Teachers has contractually promulgated a tracked policy. The recent union contract, for example, reads,

> d. In order to make certain that teachers are not frozen
> into positions which are relatively easy or difficult, the
> following procedures should be adopted in making class
> assignments (other than special assignments, such as
> RIT [Ready Improvement Teacher] IGC [Intellectually
> Gifted Children] on a particular grade level:
> (1) On each grade level, classes should be divided into
> two categories, "difficult" and "less difficult," in terms
> of reading achievement. In general, a teacher who has
> been assigned to a class in the one category for a period
> of one year should be assigned to the other category for
> the next year. Teachers who have served in a school for
> one year or longer should receive assignments for the
> next school year before June 15th.

Yet tracking is both legally and educationally unsound. A recent report on it in a sixth-grade IGC class in the Two Bridges district scores the racial implications:

Of approximately twenty-five students, eight were Chinese,
one was Black, two were Puerto Rican, and fourteen were
White. In the lowest group of the same grade, there were
roughly ten Chinese, three Black, six Puerto Rican and
one White student. This is not to suggest any conscious
discrimination against minorities. It does say that however the system works, children in the lower tracks
tend to be disproportionately from minority groups; that
the basis for the assignment to these groups is dubious.[2]

Legally, tracking has been condemned. In a landmark decision
in the federal courts in 1967, Hobson v. Hansen, Judge J. Skellev
Wright ordered the District of Columbia to halt its practice of tracking
pupils. This system, Wright declared, violated equal protection under
the Constitution. That decision was affirmed on appeal, Smuch v.
Hobson, 1969.

Educationally, a study by Harvard psychologist Robert Rosenthal
and school principal Lenore Jacobson has noted the crucial importance
of teacher attitudes in pupil performance. They discovered that teacher
expectations of pupil performance play a large role in determining that
performance. From their experiments with controlled groups they
concluded that "change in teacher expectation can lead to improved
intellectual performance."[3] The tracking system irreparably influences
teacher expectation.

Moreover, evidence is accumulating to show that heterogeneous
grouping—mixing "ability" and racial and socio-economically different
students—increases achievement levels. This seems to be true not
only for the typical white middle-class student but for the black lower-
class pupil. One such experiment in heterogeneous grouping in New
York's Upper West Side—Balanced Class Project—recorded dramatic
results. Balanced classes were organized in a series of eight schools
in the first, second, and third grades with school populations of approximately 505 white and 50 percent black and Spanish-speaking children.
The study encompassed one year between October, 1967 and April,
1968 when reading tests were administered.

The results showed significant improvement of both white and
minority children. It seriously questions the fear that "high ability"
children will deteriorate in their school work. In the second grade,
the balanced class students gained nearly a year or more, almost up
to grade level. The bilingual balanced class reading scores rose
from 1.7 to 2.5 whereas the average traced second grade pupils
registered a 1.9; black balanced class students' reading scores
increased from 2.1 to 2.8 as compared to traced black students'
score of 1.8; white increased from 2.7 to 4.1, way above the expected
grade level norm of 2.7.

The scores were equally impressive for the third grade. Bilingual average in the balanced classes was 3.7, right on the expected norm as compared to 2.4 for two nonbalanced classes in the district; black scores were 3.4 as compared to 2.5 for nonbalanced; and the white score was 5.2.

One component of the balanced class project was a formal parental role in the project. Parents took part in parent-teacher social workshops whereby Spanish-speaking black and white parents met on a continuing basis with teachers to discuss common goals. Children visited different homes in attempts to break down ethnic and racial suspicions and hostility.

An obvious conclusion on the teacher's role in heterogenous grouping was drawn; teaching children of varying "abilities" and backgrounds means more work. "In short, the effort required of teachers," the report sites, "is much greater in Balanced Classes but the results also seem much greater" (emphasis added).[4]

There are other sound educational reasons why tracking, in practice, is abominable. Many Spanish-speaking pupils for whom English is a second language often are grouped with pupils with severe emotional or behavioral problems because of their reading scores. Moreover, the level of educational content varies too greatly between the "fast" and "slow" learners rather than the pace of teaching the same materials. And, teachers with the best qualifications and the most experience are given the best classes and those with the least experience the slowest classes only to be rotated on a union contractual basis of difficult and less difficult each year. The net result is that pupils who start out in a low group remain in that tracked group.

Under the old centralized system, tracking was official policy. For example, a 1966 circular issued by the Board of Education to district superintendents and principals stated, "For purposes of proper classification and placement in grade one, teachers and supervisors should make every effort to identify intellectually gifted children by the end of kindergarten year. The judgment of teachers and supervisors should be the basis of such identification."

Officially, the central Board now disavows tracking. With respect to the Intellectually Gifted Classes in the elementary schools, the Board program has been decentralized, and authority to determine whether to have an IGC program is up to the districts. The Board has abolished the central office in charge of IGC. This is true also of the Special Progress (SP) programs on the junior high school level. Nonetheless, in practice, tracking for the most part persists and the special classes remain where the community boards have maintained the status quo.

Suspensions

Both the central and community school boards have lagged in reforming the suspension procedures. The low status of parent and child in the school system is highly evident in the suspension process. Ghetto parents have long suffered the stigma of "disruptive" children. Significantly, during the existence of Ocean Hill-Brownsville and IS 201, the governing boards and staffs of these demonstration districts were able to eliminate suspensions. However, teachers and principals in the New York City school system still rely unduly on the suspension mechansim to maintain control.

New board policy was initiated on suspensions in two areas: (1) on June 24, 1970, the new suspension policy was promulgated, and (2) on November 5, 1970, a suspension appeal procedure was adopted.

The new suspension policy entails the following: notifying parents of a pupil suspension by certified letter; a conference with the principal for all but those high school pupils who have a community superintendent hearing; the right of parents to be accompanied at conferences and hearings by at least two additional persons, including a lawyer; a hearing, must be held within five days; and the right of parents and students to cross-examine and bring witnesses. The superintendent decides on whether to return, transfer, or refer pupils. Appeals can be made to the community superintendent and then to community boards for primary students and directly to the CSB's for high school students.

The lay Board of Education and its professional staff at 110 Livingston Street are resisting grievance machinery for parents and students. In the past two years, three new programs have been formulated in response to student and parent demands: consultative councils in the high schools; new procedural rights in suspension cases; and a Parent Complaint Board, which is currently under consideration. An examination of the first two policies and of the prospects for change in the third yields little hope for reform. Parents and students remain in an essentially weak position.

The idea for consultative councils originated with the professional staff. In the spring of 1969, the acting superintendent of schools, Nathan Brown, issued guidelines for the establishment of committees in each high school to consist of parents, students, and faculty. This tentative step was taken (administrative rhetoric stated "the need for opening lines of communication to a greater degree than they had been in the past") because the high schools of the city were seething with student discontent, often erupting into riots. Subsequently, the Board, upon recommendation of the superintendent, adopted a resolution mandating that in "each high school there be established a

consultative Council consisting of representatives from the parents'
association, student body, the professional staff, community school
boards and others" to advise on "all matters affecting curriculum
above the minimum requirements under state and city statutes, the
initiation and approval of innovative programs, student rights and
responsibilities, school discipline and other appropriate areas of the
high school program." This resolution seemed to confront student
unrest.

The PEA acted as watchdog on the implementation of this new
policy. A PEA high school field team visited selected schools from
October 1969 through May 1970 and interviewed faculty, students, and
parents. The PEA issued a progress report scoring the consultative
councils as ineffective. Few students use them because they are
dominated by principals. Students are outnumbered by adults, and,
in the event an alliance develops between students and parents, the
principal can veto any decision. There is no appeal machinery.
Principals hesitate to make new policy without support from central
headquarters. The high school field team also observed that
representation on the council does not reflect a full spectrum of
community groups. Parent representatives are recruited from the
PA. Parents who have become disillusioned with the Parents'
Association—and there are many as evidenced by the small turnout
at PA meetings—are not on the council. Students on the council are
usually from the docile Student General Organization. Student
dissenters organize outside of and ignore the councils. Thus, the
consultative councils, contrary to their promising agenda, are
reinforcing the authoritative structure of the high schools.

The Board of Education considered another proposal, a Parent
Complaint Board (PCB), authored by one of its own members, Seymour
Lachman. The PCB attempts to advance parents' rights by tightening
up procedural loopholes (such as making records accessible to parents)
and providing for independent hearing examiners. However, parents
remain in a weak position vis-à-vis teachers and administrators
because the powers of the PCB, according to the proposal, would be
merely advisory. As with the consultative councils, no enforcement
machinery is provided. The plan allows for complaints in three kinds
of cases: "corporal punishment, racial and/or religious defamation
and racial and/or religious discrimination." Nothing substantively
new emerges from this proposal, since students are already protected
by law against such abuses. And the difficulty in documenting the
subtle institutional racism of which minority groups complain was
brought out in the testimony before Judge Francis E. Rivers in the
case of the "Ocean Hill-Brownsville Nineteen."

A frequent complaint of ghetto parents is that teachers aren't
teaching. Under present arrangements, when a child or parent has

a complaint, he goes to the principal in the elementary school or to
the guidance counselor in the junior and senior high school. Each
tells the parent and child that the child must learn to adjust to difficult
situations. The PCB leaves intact the present arrangement with
teachers and principals, who are accountable only to themselves. These
arrangements are contracted by the UFT and the Council of Supervisory
Associations.

So far, the clients served by the educational bureaucracy have
been severely shortchanged. Under decentralization, community
school boards do not have the power to make new policy in the critical
areas of student and parent rights. Only strong pressure from organized parent groups can force the central Board to give up some of its
power.

The Board of Education has failed to implement its reasonable
formal policy on student rights in a satisfactory fashion. One
educational observer has characterized Chancellor Scribner's student
rights policy as being "low priority." "This is the same type of
action we would expect from a traditionalist from within the Board of
Education hierarchy," she said, "and not from a supposed education
innovator brought from outside."

The New York Civil Liberties Union (NYCLU), which had worked
cooperatively with the Interim Board in preparing a code for student
rights, scores the enforcement of student rights provisions. According
to Alan Levine, head of the NYCLU student rights project, the New
York school system is a pioneer in the program. The NYCLU points
out, however, in their massively distributed handbook on student
rights (200,000 copies have been distributed, and it is in a third
printing), that the central Board is not giving away anything. Nearly
all of the rights of a student—concerning length of hair and distribution
of literature—were won in cases before the courts of the land. The
central Board, in sending out a circular on rights and responsibilities
for high school students, merely publicized these decisions and
principles.

The NYCLU finds that the new administrative machinery to
handle student rights cases is simply not working; the main fault is
that the central Board refuses to take a position on enforcing the
administrative machinery. The NYCLU is handling as many cases as
before, some 400 in 1971, with three times more inquiries and 78
court cases.

The NYCLU finds that deadlines and time limits are not adhered
to. One incident at Bushwick High School is a case in point. The
principal had censored the school newspaper and radio station, where-
upon the students, many politically conservative, resigned. However,
the matter was not adjudicated through the Board administrative
machinery until late June, after the students involved had graduated.

There is no doubt, judging by the rhetoric of Scribner's speeches, that he is aware of the high school student's alienation. Yet the central Board's actions on various cases, such as cutting of class, have revealed little of this official understanding. As a result of the time lag in the administrative cases, the NYCLU by-passed the Board machinery and began to bring cases directly to the courts.

Moreover, the NYCLU has scored the central Board for failing to enforce "98 percent" of cases. Principals disregard the Board's directives and are not held accountable for their actions. As a result, the NYCLU was forced to initiate court action against the central Board regarding its prohibition against students distributing the NYCLU student rights handibook. In June 1971 a court stipulation resolved the matter in favor of the NYCLU with the first provision stating that "The Board of Education hereby agrees to take all steps necessary including appropriate disciplinary action against school officials to enforce [distribution of] Circular 104, statement of student rights in all city high schools."

Consequently, the central staff is empowered to enforce violations of student rights perpetrated by professional school staffs. It is indicative of the dysfunction of school policy that the impetus for student rights and its enforcement have been from without the system.

THE COMMUNITY BOARDS AND CURRICULUM

Many agree with the Bundy Report that "the true measure of a structure of formal education is its effect on individual children."[5] They are dismayed by low test scores and high dropout rates and believe that drastic remedial action is needed. The 1971 reading test scores in New York City, for example, were almost uniformly lower than those of 1970 for predominantly black and Puerto Rican schools as well as white schools. A few blame this situation on problems unique to disadvantaged communities. Many more, however, tend to stress the school system's responsibility to educate its clientele. And, expectedly, they attribute considerable blame to certain school professionals—teachers who cannot teach or whose low expectations of "disadvantaged" children become self-fulfilling prophecies.

Criticism has also been directed against what is held to be an old-fashioned and irrelevant curriculum. The great importance of curriculum suggests that the CSB ought to "have the freedom to make changes in educational approaches, instructional materials, and educational objectives in order for school programs to be more closely related to the experiences of their students." This does not mean that the CSB "should discard all the traditional practices but that the community schools should have the power to modify and reconstruct the curriculum where necessary to improve its effectiveness and to strengthen its contribution to the self-worth and dignity of students."[6]

The decentralization law stipulates that the CSB's will determine matters relating to instruction of students and will select textbooks and instructional materials subject to certain conditions. The chancellor must approve textbooks and instructional materials. He will, with the approval of the city Board, establish minimum educational standards for all schools and programs. He must periodically evaluate the effectiveness of these programs and require each CSB to make annual reports on their effectiveness as well.[7] It should be emphasized that the chancellor sets minimum standards only, so it would appear that the law delegates considerable power to the community boards in the area of curriculum. Our survey of board member assessments of their power is consistent with this proposition. When asked whether they had experienced any conflicts with the city Board in the area of curriculum, about 90 percent of the CSB members responded in the negative or indicated that these conflicts were much less pronounced than those in personnel and budget. Nor did parents perceive that CSB's were unduly limited in curriculum.

What have the CSB's done with this power? Our study reveals that they have done very little to restructure the basic education program. Their major activities in the area of curriculum and education program have come under the umbrella of state and federal funds. These have been, for the most part, ancillary programs. Evaluations of these programs—which firm to hire, how much community involvement in the process—have been an issue in several districts. A number of reasons for the level of CSB activity in curriculum suggest themselves after scrutinizing these conclusions.

Basic Education Programs

Some view the open classroom as one of the more outstanding educational innovations of recent years. Although several CSB's have expressed an interest in the program, few have fleshed out their rhetoric with money. Eight districts in particular warrant mention— 3, 6, 9, 10, 12, 17, 21, and 22—for exhibiting such an interest, though no achievements have been spectacular. It is important to note that the pressure for open classrooms has often originated in the individual schools and not with the CSB's.

In District 6, for example, a Parents' Association successfully influenced its principal to try an open classroom. Neither the district office nor CSB in that district showed interest in such an innovation. The CSB in District 12 has supported open classrooms in five or six schools. District 10 has one of the few teacher-training programs in the open classroom; an old catering hall has been converted to a training center; the program is small and in absolute terms does not amount to much, but it does exist. Such training programs are essential if open classrooms are to materialize.

Several new arrangements with colleges for training open-classroom teachers have been suggested. Education instructors in the colleges typically have little experience with the open classroom, and interest in the program has often come from education students. Some colleges have thus sought the assistance of those familiar with the program in instructing education students. This approach—a course on the open classroom—has been opposed by some on the grounds that only actual field work can adequately impart the knowledge required. Others have sought to hire outside experts to administer special courses for faculty who can then teach the open-classroom approach to their students. The same objection applies here; such courses divorced from actual field experience can hardly be expected to produce experts on the open classroom.

Accordingly, the Community Resources Center, which has for some time taken an active interest in open classrooms, has proposed an internship program that would provide faculty members with actual experience. It has hired an assistant professor of education on leave for one year, placed him in an open-classroom setting, and evaluated and assisted his performance. Next year he will take a half-year leave and continue his on-the-job training. It is hoped that he will be equipped to provide similar training to others.

The open-classroom concept has been lauded by some and criticized by others. Unfortunately, the experience with it in New York City suggests that it remains, for the most part, a concept—not having been implemented to a significant degree. For the program to be meaningfully tried, adequate teacher training must be provided. Significant attempts to do this are just beginning.

What are some of the other innovative basic education programs initiated by the CSB's? In District 2, the CSB has implemented the Clinton Program: a school without walls that uses the city as campus. Students are taken on tours of the neighborhood businesses and other places. Round tables replace individual desks in the classroom, and detailed evaluations replace letter grades. The CSB has sought and accepted grants from foundations and corporations to fund the implementation of innovative aspects of the program including cost of personnel, rent, transportation, equipment, and supplies.

Also in District 2 is the experimental PS 3, which came about through the initiative of parents in the Greenwich Village area with the cooperation of CSB 2. Parents chose their principal, who was not from the list and is paid through grant money. They also selected the teachers, all of whom were city-licensed and paid through city funds. Parents also have considerable input into curriculum, which is unstructured. Plans are to spend $1.5 million to remove classroom walls to create a similarly unstructured building. About 300 children are enrolled in PS 3, which is operated on an open-admissions basis.

In the area of measuring student strengths and weaknesses truly so that schools can know what to do, CSB 2 passed the following resolution to encourage the development of improved reading test procedures:

A. The Decentralization Law requires the preparation and administration of a "comprehensive reading examination" during April and May of each year. To fulfill this requirement the Chancellor requested that the Metropolitan Achievement Test be given in all schools on March 30, 1971.

B. The administration of the Metropolitan Achievement Reading Test in District 2 on March 30, 1971 was questioned in our district on the grounds that the test (1) is discriminatory, (2) is subject to abuse through pretest coaching procedures and (3) has an adverse effect on the emotional well-being of the students.

C. A variety of suggestions have been advanced as to how the test could be changed and improved, the method of scoring [could be] revised, its administration modified and the release of test results better handled so as to meet the many valid objections raised.

RESOLVED, that to improve the administration of the test scheduled for April 1972:

1. This Board herewith instructs the Superintendent to confer with all concerned to list the changes referred to above and how they could be implemented.

2. This Board further requests the Superintendent to arrange for a meeting with the Chancellor within the next two (2) weeks to discuss implementation of these modifications on a city-wide basis.

3. The Board further directs the Community Superintendent (a) to arrange for availability of a choice of diagnostic reading tests in all schools, to be administered as needed, and (b) to develop an effective way of reporting to parents in each school.

4. The Superintendent is requested to report regarding this matter at the next public meeting so that the Board may consider further immediate action.

The mini-school of Joan of Arc JHS in District 3 also represents a noteworthy change by a CSB. The students have been selected at random with the prior consent of their parents. Teachers were chosen from those regularly licensed teachers who volunteered for the experiment. The curriculum is loosely structured; as in the Clinton Program in District 2, emphasis is on the city as a campus. Comparisons of students in the program with those in a regular school setting indicate the former have a higher level of motivation to learn. Parents have been encouraged to participate in the program—to help with administrative matters and to observe what happens in the classroom. The school was temporarily located on Manhattan's East Side, a considerable distance from where the parents lived. It has since been moved to a storefront in the neighborhood, and parental involvement in the school has been increasing.

CSB 3 is presently pursuing initiatives that may result in future changes in the basic education program. In 1971, District 3 submitted a proposal to the federal government under Title III for a planning grant that would allow the district to work out a way of setting up alternate schools. This proposal was rejected at the time. Recently the federal government approached the district offering to fund that planning grant. The amount of money involved is between $50,000 and $100,000. The proposal would allow a single complex (IS 44) to work up the exact steps involved and the exact costs of an alternate school plan within that complex.

In last year's education budget, Chancellor Scribner set aside a large sum of money and set up a new department called the Learning Cooperative headed by Dr. Edythe Gaines. CSB 3 sought and secured money to be used for the planning of basic restructuring of schools to improve learning within the IS 88 complex. The community superintendent of District 3 and his staff visited the Calhoun School, a long-established prominent private school, and found a unique teaching method being used. He and the CSB believe it could benefit the children in the district and have proposed using state monies so some of the district's teaching staff can learn it and help teach it to other members of the staff.

The CSB in District 9 received Office of Economic Opportunity (OEO) money for a performance contract, and the board contracted with Tarkenton Ventures of Athens, Georgia, which placed heavy emphasis on teaching machines. Most observers agree that the program, tested at JHS 117, failed. Teachers from the beginning opposed the project. Albert Shanker, the president of the UFT, wrote a newspaper column blaming the CSB and the community superintendent and OEO for the failure of the experiment, which he thought ill-conceived. The CSB and the superintendent blamed teachers for not keeping the machines in repair. Although the project failed, it does represent an attempt at innovation.

Of particular interest in District 12 are the Caleb Gattegno schools, which are federally funded. The schools attempt to build on what children already know. Traditional approaches have been swept aside; for example, in the Gattegno method, students are taught algebra before elementary arithmetic. Teachers in the program were required to undergo special training. They eat with the children and take turns serving food in the cafeteria. Dr. Gattegno meets with educational experts weekly to discuss the program's progress; they spend one day a week monitoring classrooms. This program is certainly innovative and is being watched closely by people in education.

These and other programs and initiatives in basic education are impressive. But they seem to be the exception, not the rule. Most CSB's have not been active in this area.

Ancillary Programs

The CSB's have been more active, however, in the area of programs that do not affect the central portion of the curriculum presented to the student. Although some of the basic education programs are funded by state and federal money, most of the ancillary programs are so funded. Because many of these programs are dealt with in the Title I section, our treatment here will be brief.

Most CSB's have continued experimental and innovative ancillary programs, such as special reading and math programs, educational assistants to aid underachievers, after-school study centers, etc. The educational assistants work with small groups and individual children who are underachievers, usually in the first and second grades. They also relieve teachers of some clerical and administrative duties so the teachers can devote more time to instruction, as well as help prepare materials and assist in other class activities.

Several districts have special reading programs similar to the Reading Skills Centers and JHS Reading Laboratories in District 22, where the reading centers in four schools are equipped with from 20 to 25 individual carrels each, containing "Junior Controlled Readers." Each student is programmed individually and works at his own speed. The reading teacher pretests the student at the beginning and tests at the end of the semester to find the gain achieved and also gives individual instruction as needed. This program, which handles pupils in grades four, five, and six, supplements the regular corrective reading program, which only handles pupils in grades one, two, and three. The JHS Reading Laboratories, operating in two schools, run on the same principles.

CSB 22 has also established a diagnostic center in the district office to serve children who have severe learning problems and are

unresponsive to corrective procedures in regular classes and corrective reading rooms. These students come to the center for testing,
evaluation, and programing for remediation. They are taught individually or in small groups. Corrective techniques are outlined for the
use of home schools as well. CSB 22 and other boards have continued
and have sought to expand these and related programs. The Strengthening Early Childhood (SEC) program, sponsored by the UFT, is in
several districts, and many CSB's consider it important. CSB 2, for
example, has endorsed the program in strong terms:

> The experience has contributed substantially to the
> children's academic achievement, their social develop-
> ment and their positive attitudes toward school. Parents
> of the participating children have, through program
> activities, been increasingly able to participate actively
> in school and community matters. In many instances,
> these programs have made it possible for parents to
> find employment in both business and the schools.

Another notable UFT-developed program is the More Effective
Schools program. This program, however, seems to be losing
enthusiasm in several districts. The UFT reported, for example,
that 6 districts this year eliminated 9 More Effective Schools and 6
districts voted to cut funds for 11 More Effective Schools. The
budgetary situation has obviously added to the negative impact on this
program. Some argue that, although MES is a good program in itself,
it is simply too costly for the few students that can be involved.
Several districts have developed and implemented new ancillary
programs. CSB 22, for example, initiated and seeks to expand an Environmental and Multi-Media Center. In this program, a mini-museum,
exhibits, live animals, and indoor and outdoor laboratories are visited
by classes in grades two to five, consisting of the greatest number of
underachievers, accompanied by their teachers. Orientation sessions
at the home schools before the visits prepare the children for their
lab and field experiences, during which they collect and observe
aquatic and land organisms. It is expected that these experiences
will improve the students' manipulative skills and develop problem-
solving abilities. It is hoped that many children having difficulty
learning to read from books will profit as they develop an interest in
learning through exciting firsthand experiences in science and ecology.
Teachers and students alike will probably benefit from a see, hear,
smell, and touch approach to ecology problems. The multi-media
facilities give students a chance to research topics in which they have
become interested while at the Environmental Center, providing
motivation for reading for the underachiever.

Other districts, especially 3, 10, 12, 13, and 17, have adopted new ancillary programs, which supplement the basic curriculum.

EVALUATION OF EDUCATION PROGRAMS

The decentralization law stipulates that the chancellor must require each CSB to make annual reports on the effectiveness of their educational programs. In part, this is accomplished by conveying to the chancellor the results of the mandatory reading tests referred to above. In addition to this, some CSB's have submitted general reports of the programs in their district, which really does not amount to an evaluation. So, in effect, virtually no systematic evaluation of some basic education programs has been undertaken.

A different situation prevails for Title I and state urban education programs. The federal Elementary and Secondary Education Act requires an annual evaluation of every project funded by Title I. A similar requirement for evaluation of all state-funded programs is found in the New York State Education Law. All proposals for evaluation of these programs must be submitted to the chancellor for final approval and must be voted on by the city Board at its public meeting.

District 14 in Brooklyn worked out an interesting program, which included both parent and community evaluators. The primary concerns were with reading and writing and math. For every teacher in a class, there were four paraprofessionals and one tutor in each complex for the summer program. There was a training period of one hour a day for the paraprofessionals and teachers. A total of some 1,500 community people were employed. Besides this, the Institute for Educational Development (IED) was hired as a consultant, and it in turn hired eight or nine community people to work as an evaluation team to be supervised by trained evaluators. The community people went into the schools each day, and the teacher to be evaluated would not know when the team would be visiting. Most of those involved with this program agreed that it was successful.

One of the major accomplishments of such a program was bringing teachers into contact with community people. District 14's program of community evaluation served to recognize the community's right to scrutinize this process. It did so in a way that indicated that the demand for public influence in curriculum matters does not mean a rejection of professionalism. An evaluation process similar to this occurred in District 17 as well.

Very few evaluation programs, however, have sought to involve the community. Many CSB's seem to have a deep seated suspicion of community involvement in this area and tend to defer to the expertise of the professionals. For example, many people in District 28 did not know the CSB had submitted an evaluation proposal for their state-funded programs. Upon learning of the proposal, parents managed to push through an amendment to include the training and use of parent evaluators to assist the evaluation team.[8] The evaluation of certain state-funded programs in District 16 completely excludes the community in the process, as do most evaluation programs.

It is one thing to evaluate a program and another to use the evaluations effectively. For example, in District 5 a few innovative programs have been developed in the area of curriculum. A day-care program and multimedia programs were considered quite successful. Several parents lobbied for these programs but were incensed the following year, when the community superintendent, asked what he would like to see in that district's curriculum, responded that he would be satisfied if the minimum required program could be met. The fact that annual reports on educational effectiveness are required by the city Board does not mean that they will be heeded. It would seem that inclusion of the community in more aspects of the evaluation process might facilitate this feedback. Some public pressure, at least, would exist in favor of using the evaluations effectively.

CONCLUSION

Neither parents nor CSB members interviewed saw the area of curriculum as the most significant failure of the school boards. Our analysis suggests, however, that the CSB's have not been very active in curriculum and education programs. They have done least in the area of basic education programs and most in that of ancillary programs.

The discrepancy in levels of activity between basic education programs and ancillary programs can be explained with little difficulty. The latter are very often federally funded, and there has been a court case in this area. The New York State supreme court ruled that CSB 3 had the right to make decisions locally about the use of federal funds that are allocated to poverty areas. The law, it was reasoned, turned over selection of Title I programs to the CSB's within certain state and federal guidelines. There is perhaps more room for local initiative with respect to ancillary programs than there is for basic education programs, which are most often paid for through the general tax levy funds.

Several factors combine to explain the general inactivity of the CSB's in the area of curriculum and education programs. Perhaps most important are the limits placed on the boards by the UFT contract. For example, that contract requires that in a period of budget cuts specially trained and experienced substitute teachers be excessed before regular teachers. This provision can have a disastrous impact on the educational program of a district. CSB 3 found that it would cripple the district's "open classroom" program if honored, because that program's success hinged on using a large number of substitutes. The District 3 board consequently sued the city Board, but the court turned down the district's petition and placed the matter in the lap of State Education Commissioner Ewald Nyquist, who ruled against the district. Seniority continues to be honored in all cases, even if the school program suffers.

The UFT contract has limited other districts as well. A CSB member in District 25 reports that several clashes with the UFT have occurred in that district. Some principals seeking flexibility in scheduling teachers found it necessary to put 34 or 35 students in a given class in order that the general educational program run smoothly. The UFT filed grievances because the number of pupils violated the contract. Generally, the UFT is most concerned that the contract be met. The UFT delegate in District 25, for example, lobbied for a special classroom for disruptive children handled by an extra teacher. The CSB was interested in including various agencies in the community to assist in this program, but the UFT would not support it in this. Once the special classroom and teacher had been provided, its interest in the program ceased.

Some have viewed the Council of Supervisory Associations as an obstacle to CSB activity in curriculum as well. Few will dispute the importance of the educational leadership provided by a school principal. This was perhaps less true before the change in the law (supervisors are no longer tenured) and the new city Board policy following the Mansfield decision (supervisors are no longer necessarily from the list). The presence of these factors goes far to explain the lack of change in principals and acting principals; up to 1972, the CSB's changed only 100. The change in the law and the new city Board policy have weakened the CSA and opened the gates to change for the CSB's.

Even if it were not for limits imposed by the contract, many CSB's might still be inactive in curriculum. Several CSB members interviewed tended to view this area as appropriate only to "professionals." They reason that, because they lack technical training in the area, they had better not tamper with it, lest they wreck the whole ship. The corollary is that, when a CSB dominated by members sharing this perspective does act on curriculum, emphasis is on developing procedures (which often is simply a euphemism for delay or inaction) and "feeling its way" before exerting itself with any confidence in such a new and uncharted domain.

A recently published study by the Institute for Community Studies suggests that a lack of defined educational goals can be as responsible for ineffective programs as a CSB's need to "feel its way."[9] In fact, the inability of the CSB's to deal with the issue of educational goals, to search for a coherent philosophy of education, is probably their basic failure in this regard.

The attitude of CSB 30, summed up by the chairman of its curriculum committee, is illustrative of how CSB's can abdicate their leadership responsibilities in this area: "It is not our role to restructure curriculum for the district. Our role is advisory and consultative. The individual schools should work with their principals to decide what they want to do and we will give . . . as much help as possible."

The predecessors to the community school boards were the 25 appointed local district boards created in 1961. "The activation of such local boards was, in part, a recognition of the inadequacy of both one city wide board and a system too overcentralized to respond to local needs."[1] However, the activation of a system of district boards did not mean a change in the direction of education policy, or an inclusion of a new group in decision-making. The local boards became community buffers taking the abuse meant for a central board. The local boards have been described as bodies with "no real determination in school policy. Generally, they . . . hold hearings and discuss narrow local issues, yet they have not had the authority to resolve local problems. . . . Officially, the boards rarely act as a body: members are more prone to voice personal views on issues. Local boards do not have the information or facility, much less the authority, to follow through on matters that affect policy."[2]

Beyond the creation of six additional districts in 1965, this administrative decentralization effort produced no real change in the operation of the school system. The effects and accomplishments of the 31 boards were minimal. Budgeting and personnel policy continued to be a central Board function with local boards having no input into decision-making.

Despite the lack of community input into the schools, "the distance between school and community became a prime educational issue only after the schools began noticeably to fail in delivering a satisfactory product to large numbers of pupils, especially low-income urban racial minorities."[3] At first, the apparent answer to black failure was school integration. A mixing of white and black students was looked to as the route to ending the problems of black children. But the system and the public resisted any major movement toward integration.

It was out of the failure to integrate the schools that the move-ment for community control of the schools was born. Frustrated by a system that refused to integrate, black parents turned toward control of their schools as a prerequisite to achieving quality education. "Isaiah Robinson suggested almost as [a] joke that since white children would not be sent into Harlem schools and black children were not being invited downtown in any meaningful numbers, maybe the blacks had better accept segregation and run their own schools."[4]

On the first of July, 1970, 279 local school board members assumed office in the 31 local school boards. Thus, the educational system was legally decentralized. Theoretically, decentralization should lead to more representative and responsive local boards with sufficient power to control local educational policy. The election of local school boards did not achieve that end.

The typical community school board member is a white male of the Jewish or Catholic faith, a middle-class professional, with at least two children attending a nonpublic school and living in his district for approximately nine years.

In contrast, the typical school board member in the three demon-stration districts (Ocean Hill-Brownsville, IS 201, and Two Bridges) that had been created in 1967 and abolished under the 1969 decentral-ization legislation more approached the model of a representative local board. The average demonstration district governing board member was a female, a high school graduate with poverty-worker background, with children in the public schools.

The reason that the newly elected community school boards failed to include substantially the urban poor in their membership was that the school decentralization law and accompanying election procedures were poorly designed to accomplish these purposes. The results of the school board elections show that of the 279 board mem-bers elected throughout the city 16.8 percent (47) were black; 10.8 percent (30), Puerto Rican; 72 percent (201), white; and .4 percent (1), of Chinese origin.

BOARD MEMBER PROFILE

Occupation: 63.8 percent of board members held professional, technical, or managerial positions; 10.3 percent were employed as paraprofessionals or by poverty agencies; 5.3 percent were clergymen; 16.6 percent were housewives; and 4.0 percent were employed as labor-ers, mechanics, or other quasi-skilled or unskilled low-paying jobs.

Age: The average age of the members was 41.8, ranging from 18 years to 68 years.

Family size: 81.9 percent of the local school board members were married, having an average of 2.2 children per household; 46.8

percent of them had children in the public schools; 53.2 percent of
them sent their children to parochial schools with 8.5 percent among
this latter group sending their preschool children also to parochial
schools.

Residence: 11.8 percent had resided in the districts in which
they won for less than five years; 31.2 percent had lived in districts
for from five to fifteen years, while more than half (57.0 percent) had
resided in their districts for over fifteen years.

Religious identification: 36.0 percent were Jewish; 50.6 percent
Catholic; 11.2 percent Protestant.

RACIAL-ETHNIC DISTRIBUTION

In six districts (2, 11, 18, 23, 27, and 28) with a population of
black and Puerto Rican pupils ranging from 30 to 48 percent, only 5
of the 54 school board members were nonwhite. In 12 districts that
are predominantly black or Puerto Rican (over 85 percent of the school
population) only 6 (4, 5, 7, 9, 16, and 23) had boards with a majority of
black or Puerto Rican members. In contrast, the other six districts
(1, 12, 13, 14, 17, and 19) had no less than five and as many as seven
white members distributed as follows: five each in Districts 1 and 5,
six each in Districts 12, 14, and 17, and seven in District 19. Thus,
in the 18 districts mentioned, only 64 local school board members out
of a total of 162 were black and Puerto Rican with 98 being white. A
further breakdown of the figures shows that a little more than 56 percent (44 out of a total of 78) of the minority members of the local school
boards in a city-wide distribution were concentrated in 6 districts (4,
5, 7, 9, 16, and 23), while the remaining 34 minority members were
scattered throughout the remaining 25 districts. Of these, 10 districts—
15, 28, 20, 21, 22, 23, 24, 26, 27, and 31, with 66 percent, 29 percent,
22 percent, 11 percent, 33 percent, 29 percent, 15 percent, 32 percent,
and 11 percent minority school population respectively—elected all-
white school boards. This is a significant factor since even in districts
where the white school population is as low as .1 percent (District 23
in Brooklyn) one white was elected to the board; District 1 with 9
percent, District 4 with 2 percent, District 7 with 2 percent, District
12 with 5 percent, District 13 with 5 percent, District 14 with 10 percent, and District 16 with 9 percent elected six, three, two, six, five,
six, and two white members respectively. Furthermore, there was
only one district (5 in Manhattan) where no whites were elected to
the community boards. In contrast, there were ten local school boards
with no minority group members.

Five sections of the decentralization act had, more than the
others, significant impact in determining the eventual outcome of the

elections and the composition of all 31 community school boards. They
were (1) districting, (2) nomination, (3) registration and voting, (4)
powers of the local school boards, and (5) the electoral mechanism of
proporational representation. No interpretation of the outcome of the
elections can be meaningful without a discussion of these variables,
and, while succinct analysis will follow presently, it is appropriate
first to look into the general premises of the selection process.

Despite a lack of community involvement in the selection of new
board members, there has been a slight increase in the number of
black and Puerto Rican board members. In 1970, there were 47 blacks
board members. By May, 1972, there were 55. Puerto Rican members
on community school boards increased during the same period from
30 to 38. Only the number of white members has declined, from 201
to 175. There is still only one Oriental member in the entire city.
(See Table 12.)

Districts that had vacancies continued to make and implement
policy in their areas. District 30 made many decisions with only
eight members. So did Districts 6 and 17.

In addition to some boards, functioning without a complete nine-
member complement, several boards have had an unusually high rate
of board member absenteeism at public meetings. At least two districts,
1 and 6, have had to cancel public meetings for lack of a quorum. In
both districts, canceled meetings had at least 150 parents present.
District 6 in Manhattan was unable to start three of its public meetings
in the 1971-72 school year as only three members of the CSB were in
attendance. Districts 28 and 31 rarely have all members of the board
present at public meetings. In the former, two and three absences
were common at each meeting. Most of the parents interviewed for
this study pointed to the frequent absence of board members at meetings
as a disappointing fact of life with their board.

TABLE 12

Composition of Community School Boards,
1969, 1972

Date	Puerto Rican	Black	White	Oriental	Vacancies
1969	30	47	201	1	—
May, 1972	38	55	175	1	10

Source: Boulton H. Demas, The School Elections (New York:
Institute for Community Studies, 1971).

There is a necessary connection between the incorporation of a school board, the way it is organized, and its ability to create change or produce momentum in educational policy. In an attempt to evaluate the progress of the decentralized school boards in New York City, we have found that the community school boards fall into three categories: (1) status quo boards, (2) active boards, and (3) change-agent boards.

A status quo board makes no attempt to deviate from the established ways of doing things. Its conduct is guided by a narrow interpretation of the rules of the Board of Education and the decentralization law. It views the central Board's role as primary. Parental involvement is negligible, deference to professionals is common, and personnel procedures are unchanged.

An active board is one that takes limited action in adjusting school policy and has had some success in a few areas. It sees its own role and that of parents and local residents as supplementary to standards and procedures set by school professionals.

A change-agent board is characterized by a high degree of parental involvement in the hiring of teachers and principals, the selection of other key personnel for the district, the granting of tenure to civil service personnel, the deviation from established personnel practices illustrated by hiring pedagogical personnel whose names do not appear on the ranked lists of the Board of Examiners, the degree to which it seeks to inform the community, the frequency with which notices of open public meetings are circulated, the frequency of public hearings, the hiring of its own new district superintendent upon its assuming office, and innovation of educational output.

CSB-SUPERINTENDENT RELATIONS

Many analysts of school politics agree that the most important decision made by a school board is the selection of the superintendent. Evaluation of a superintendent's performance demands a high level of communication between the school board and its administration. Should the communication system between them be lax, or break down, the board may lose control of policy and the implementation of decisions. The board must rely on its chief administrative officer for information about the schools, and it is this information that provides the basis for decision-making. In this connection, the findings of Neal Gross, in his study of superintendents in New England is corroborative:

More school board members expressed dissatisfaction with the level of information about the schools and educational practices of their board than with any other aspect or characteristic which could affect school board functioning. Only

38% said they were very satisfied with their board's level
of information, and the rest expressed lesser degrees of
satisfaction, 16% of them expressing clear dissatisfaction
on this score.[5]

Thus, the relationship that exists between a community school
board and its superintendent can be shown to fall into three mutually
exclusive categories: (1) constructive or cooperative, (2) dominative,
and (3) conflictual. These categories respectively complement the
change-agent, active, and status quo school boards.

School boards that hired new community superintendents
generally seek a cooperative relationship with their superintendents.
The superintendent is more likely to keep the school board well informed of his actions, and he works cooperatively with the board,
seeking neither to usurp the policy-making powers of the board nor to
allow himself to become the board's puppet. Such an attitude becomes
conducive to the minimization of conflict and results in increased
policy output. Analysis of interviews in the 31 decentralized districts
in New York City shows that only 23 percent of the school board
members said that their superintendent kept them well informed.
Interestingly, those CSB respondents who answered "Yes" to the
question "Do you, in general, approve of what your district superintendent is doing?" also replied that they have had frequent contacts with
their district superintendents, that he makes suggestions to them for
their activities, and that the CSB also makes suggestions to him that
he follows.

School boards 3 and 13—the only two change-agent boards in the
city—fall into this category. By avoiding conflict a good part of the
time and minimizing domination, change-agent school boards create
the climate for community participation with a resultant increase in
policy output. On the contrary, one pervasive characteristic of status
quo school boards is that they rehired the incumbent superintendents.
Moreover, in very many cases, they have gone further and renewed
the contracts of these superintendents even if educational policy
output was negligible. In those cases the boards are virtually non-
functioning, relying on the superintendent to run the district.* A few
of the status quo boards seem to use their superintendents as fronts
for a strong board chairman who actually makes all policy. The
board interferes, meddles, and obstructs attempts at reform initiated
by the community superintendent and/or other school officials. The

---

*This is a pattern observed in almost all school board studies
in suburban and urban communities.

result is frequent conflict and little program output. "If he must spend much of his time," says Gross, "anticipating threats and developing strategies to deal with them, [the superintendent] will not have much time left to administer the schools efficiently and work with his staff to develop and carry out an effective educational program."[6]

For example, in the more than two years since CSB 23 assumed office, the superintendency changed hands three times. On one occasion, the appointment lasted for only one month. The most recent community superintendent, Dr. Bobby Ray Johnson, has weathered the vicissitudes of that office for at least five months. The high attrition rate of super- intendents in this district is attributable to the domination of the board's chairman, assemblyman and attorney Samuel Wright. One administrator said that Wright controls the activities of the community superintendent and the school board. Communication with the superintendent is done through secretaries and other intermediaries. His control of the school board is exemplified by his preemptory ending of discussions. "Fre- quently," says this respondent, "the CSB would be discussing an item, Sam would walk out for some twenty minutes, then return and ask for a vote on the question. He usually wins."[7] Allegations are made that allocations for education are squandered on the acquirement of plant facilities owned by Wright's political supporters and protégés. In one week, the New York Amsterdam News, The New York Post, and The New York Times scored him on these allegations. Specifically, the newspapers alleged that Wright needs a community superintendent of record only because the superintendent's signature is necessary on the vouchers for what some claim to be the bogus disbursements that Wright orders from time to time. It is hardly likely that this erratic change in chief administrators can lead to the development of innovation in educational policy.

Several active boards appointed new superintendents upon assum- ing power. CSB 17 is an example. Dr. Charles I. Schonhaut was hired when the school board assumed office. The district's parents and residents were invited to the screening of the top five candidates, and, though the final selection rested with the new school board, the com- munity was in accord with Schonhaut's selection. He earned the respect of both the community and the school board with the result that program output during his administration has been good and conflict between the CSB and the community superintendent kept to a minimum. In this climate, the striving for educational excellence is amply rewarded.

COMMUNITY PARTICIPATION

The relationship between the community and its school board as established under the decentralization law is limited to two areas:

(1) public hearings prior to the submission of proposals to the chancellor for construction, remodeling, or enlargement of schools under its jurisdiction, and (2) public hearings in budgetary and fiscal processes. In this regard, the law states that "Each community board, <u>after public hearings</u> on the estimates prepared by its community superintendent, shall submit to the chancellor estimates . . . for the performance of its functions during the next year" (Section 5690). The second mandate of the decentralization law concerning the relationship between the CSB and the community is that all decisions of the CSB must be voted upon at open public meetings.

Despite the incorporation of the community's role into the law, the community at large does not become involved in the making of educational policy. Involvement depends on active organized groups—religious (the Catholic Church, the JDL), poverty (OEO-sponsored organizations), political (NEGRO), and the PA's. The PA's are the most intimately involved; the influence of the other groups is sporadic and localized. In addition, since public hearings on budget are held at least once yearly and since public meetings are usually attended by parents with public school children, to speak of community participation is, in essence, to speak of parent participation.

CSB-PARENT RELATIONS

Section § 2590-d of the decentralization law dealing with the by-laws of the community school boards spells out the minimum CSB-parent relationship, mandating (1) that there shall be a parents' association or a parent-teachers' association in each school under its jurisdiction, and (2) that the board, the community superintendent, and the principal of each school have regular communication with all PA's and PTA's within the community district to the end that such associations are provided with full factual information pertaining to matters of pupil achievement, including but not limited to annual reading scores, comparison of the achievement of pupils in comparable grades and schools, as well as the record of achievement of the same children as they progress through the school; provided, however, that such record and scores shall not be disclosed in a manner that will identify individual pupils.

The Board of Education, in its booklet "Parent Associations and the Schools," expands on the CSB's obligation in this area, suggesting that the CSB's (1) inform the PA's about procedures and timetables for standardized testing in a way understandable to parents; (2) carry out their powers in frequent prior consultation with their respective PA's or PTA's; (3) inform the PA's or PTA's as to the criteria used for evaluating teachers and administrative staff plus other procedural

TABLE 13

Profile of Districts and Community School Boards

Districts Grouped by Racial Make-Up of School Population	Communities Included	Noncirculation of Public Meeting Notices	District Newspapers	Percent of Eligible Voters Who Elected Board
Black-Puerto Rican				
1	Lower East Side			15.0
3	Lower and Upper Park West		x	8.3
4	East Harlem			9.0
5	Central Harlem			5.6
6	Inwood-Washington Heights			12.9
7	South Bronx			9.8
8	Clason Point-Throgs Neck			13.5
9	Concourse			7.4
12	Morrisania			7.2
13	Brooklyn Heights-Bedford Stuyvesant			7.7
14	Williamsburg-Greenpoint			17.3
15	South Brooklyn-Park Slope		x	14.0
16	Bushwick-Ridgewood			8.0
17	Crown Heights-Flatbush		x	7.7
19	East New York	x		13.3
23	Brownsville			4.9
29	Queens Village-Springfield Gardens		x	16.6
White				
18	Canarsie-East Flatbush			17.4
20	Bay Ridge-Bensonhurst			18.9
21	Gravesend-Coney Island			14.8
22	Midwood-Sheepshead Bay		x	17.8
24	Maspeth-Middle Village		x	14.8
25	Flushing-College Point			19.3
26	Bayside-Douglaston			22.0
27	Richmond Hill-South Rockaway			16.3
30	Astoria-Woodside	x	x	13.4
31	Entire borough of Richmond	x		18.2
Mixed				
2	Lower West Side-East Midtown	x	x	9.0
10	Fordham-Riverdale			15.6
11	Williamsbridge-North Bronx			15.2
28	Forest Hills-Jamaica			12.2

	Superintendents					Parental Involvement		
Districts	Old	New	Rehired	Resigned	Remarks	Formal Procedures	No Formal Procedures	Ratification of Parents' Choice of Personnel
Black-Puerto Rican								
1	x			x			x	No
3		x	x			x		Yes
4		x	x			x		Yes
5								
6							x	Yes
7	x			x		x		Yes
8		x	x			x		Yes
9		x				x		Yes
12					Unique	x		Yes
13			x			x		Yes
14							x	No
15			x			x		Yes
16								Yes
17			x			x		Yes
19			x				x	No
23		x			3 resigned		x	No
29								
White								
18								
20	x							
21								No
22	x	x		x		x		Yes
24								No
25								No
26								No
27								No
30		x				x		Yes
31								No
Mixed								
2						x		Yes
10						x		Yes
11							x	No
28								No

(continued)

TABLE 13 (continued)

Districts	Rank of Voter Turnout	Composition of CSB				Vacancies	Pupil Population	Ethnic Percentage of Pupil Population			
		B	W	PR	O			PR	B	W	O
Black-Puerto Rican											
1	12	1	3	3		2	12,715	71	15	9	5
3	24	2	4	2		1	15,102	31	50	18	1
4	23	3	1	5		0	15,523	65	33	2	
5	30	7	0	2		0	16,133	16	82	1	1
6	19	0	5	1		3	14,410	38	36	25	
7	21	2	2	5		0	23,847	66	32	2	
8	16	1	7	1		0	22,640	42	30	28	
9	28	4	2	3		0	25,670	40	45	15	
12	29	5	3	1		0	25,005	57	38	5	
13	27	5	3	1		0	17,995	22	73	5	
14	7	1	2	6			19,310	63	27	10	
15	15	0	9	0		0	18,517	49	17	34	
16	25	4	1	2		2	30,818	31	60	9	
17	26	5	4	0		0	16,824	19	69	12	
19	18	1	7	1		0	25,276	33	50	17	
23	31	7	0	2		0	17,545	28	71	1	
29	8	1	7	0		0	18,254	4	57	39	
White											
18	6	0	9	0		0	13,280	7	31	62	
20	3	0	9	0		0	18,868	10	11	79	
21	13	0	9	0		0	20,194	8	11	81	
22	5	1	7	0		1	19,528	2	9	89	
24	13	0	9	0		0	15,382	16	13	71	
25	2	1	8	0		0	18,503	4	9	87	
26	1	0	9	0		0	14,236	2	13	85	
27	9	0	9	0		0	22,720	4	28	67	
30	17	0	9	0		0	18,007	14	20	66	
31	4	0	9	0		0	26,624	3	8	89	
Mixed											
2	22	1	6	1	1	0	14,183	31	13	37	19
10	10	0	8	1		0	16,496	22	21	57	
11	11	0	8	1		0	16,044	12	33	55	
28	20	3	6	0		0	17,814	6	41	53	

Districts	Information			Degree of Effectiveness of Title I Advisory Committees			
	Good	Adequate	Insufficient	Effective	Noneffective	#School	#Title I
Black-Puerto Rican							
1			x		x	20	20
3	x			x		23	23
4		x		x		22	22
5			x			23	23
6		x			x	14	10
7		x			x	24	21
8		x			x	25	14
9			x		x	26	22
12			x		x	22	20
13	x			x		22	22
14	x				x	27	27
15		x		x		25	21
16		x		x		27	27
17		x		x		17	15
19		x			x	29	28
23		x			x	23	23
29	x					26	8
White							
18		x				18	5
20	x				x	30	23
21			x			29	5
22	x				x	27	0
24		x			x	24	3
25			x		x	28	0
26	x				x	29	0
27	x				x	31	8
30			x		x	25	8
31			x		x	44	10
Mixed							
2		x		x		28	15
10		x			x	24	7
11		x			x	27	0
28		x			x	28	8

(continued)

TABLE 13 (continued)

Districts	Church Influential Yes	No	Community Corporation Yes	No	Group Conflict BL-W	BL-PR	PR-W	UFT Influence Yes	No
Black Puerto Rican									
1		x	x				x	x	
3		x	x						x
4		x	x			x			x
5		x	x						x
6		x		x	x				x
7		x	x			x			x
8		x	x			x	x		x
9		x	x			x		x	
12		x	x					x	
13		x	x					x	
14		x	x		x			x	
15	x			x	x			x	
16		x		x					x
17		x	x						x
19		x		x		x			x
23		x		x				x	
29	x			x	x			x	
White									
18				x				x	
20		x		x					x
21	x			x				x	
22	x							x	
24	x			x					x
25	x			x				x	
26	x			x				x	
27	x		x					x	
30	x			x	x			x	
31	x			x				x	
Mixed									
2	x			x				x	
10	x			x				x	
11	x			x					x
28		x		x	x			x	

Sources: United Parents' Association; The New York Times, March 8, 1972; interviews with CSB members and community residents.

information including timetables for evaluation; and (4) inform the PA's and PTA's of vacancies in the matter of the selection of principals, acting principals, assistant principals, and acting assistant principals within a reasonable period of time after their occurrence.

Although the legal relationship of the CSB's to the parents' groups is consultative, parents have been called upon by several boards as active participants in certain areas of policy-making. In some districts parent groups have insisted on a more direct role in the development of programs and the selection of personnel. Almost uniformly, in change-agent districts, principal selection vacancies were filled by candidates who were the choice of PA's.

As a result, districts can be characterized by high, medium, or low parental involvement. School boards with high parental involvement encourage official and direct parent participation in such policy areas as personnel selection, review of Title I programs, and evaluation. School boards that encourage medium parental participation use both parents and the community sparingly and only in a consultative way. Low-parental-involvement boards often actively seek to exclude parents.

Parental involvement in the area of personnel has been documented earlier, but, because parents and other residents possess more formal power in the area of Title I programs, it can serve as a significant measure of the community boards' policy toward parental involvement. To highlight the relationship between the creation of functioning Title I advisory committees and the achievement levels of minority children, a brief review is in order.

Before decentralization, Title I funds were controlled by central headquarters, but many persons complained that the commingling of funds diverted the benefits from the children for whom the monies were originally intended. To dramatize the problem of commingled funds further, Peat, Marwick, and Mitchell, a large firm of certified public accountants, was retained by the Board of Education in 1969. One of its mandates was to suggest ways of restructuring parts of the Board's accounting system. Addressing itself to the central Board's auditing system, Peat, Marwick, and Mitchell said, in part, that its examination "did not provide the expected information because we could not distinguish among the expenditure of tax levy funds, Title I funds and state urban education funds." The firm recommended that "the board should seriously consider making changes in its present accounting system . . . because of a lack of information relating to the expenditures of the programs studied. Without such information, the board finds it extremely difficult to demonstrate the total impact of Title I funds upon the children the funds are intended to serve."[8] Rather than being used to develop programs beyond the general curriculum, monies were commingled with the tax-levy funds to meet the financial needs of the entire city's public school system.

In 1970 Congress amended Title I to provide that, prior to receiving a grant, a local educational agency must make the application and all pertinent documents available to parents and the general public (20 U.S., Congress, § 241e). Congress also authorized the Commissioner of Education to promulgate criteria designed to ensure that Title I programs be planned and operated in consultation with parents of the children to be served, that parents have an opportunity to present their views, and that there be adequate dissemination of program plans and evaluations to parents and the public (20 U.S., Congress, § 1231d). On April 27, 1971 the U.S. Office of Education, acting pursuant to 20 U.S., Congress, § 1231d, published proposed regulations designed to assure parental involvement in the planning, operation, and evaluation of Title I programs (36 Fed. Reg. 7861-63).

Parental involvement at the local level was deemed to be an important means of increasing the effectiveness of the programs. The new rules required every future application for a Title I grant to include specific plans for disseminating complete information about past and present Title I programs, including evaluations, to parents and the general public and for making full texts of applications and all other pertinent documents available on request. Future applications were required to describe how parents were consulted and involved in the planning of the project and to set forth specific plans for their continuing involvement. Each local educational agency was required, prior to the submission of any future application, to establish a council consisting entirely of parents not employed by the local agency or to designate for that purpose an existing group in which such parents would constitute the majority. Each future application was required to contain sufficient information to enable the state educational agency to make a number of determinations, including the following: (1) each member of the parent council had been furnished copies of federal and state laws, regulations, and guidelines; (2) the parent council had been provided with the plans for future projects together with a description of the planning process; (3) the parent council had had adequate opportunity to consider the available information on the special educational needs of the children to be served, to make recommendations as to meeting those needs, to review evaluations of prior programs, and to submit comments to the state educational agency at the time of submitting the application; and (4) all parents had had an opportunity to present their views concerning the application to the appropriate school personnel.

On June 29, 1971 Chancellor Scribner wrote to the chairman and superintendents of all community school boards concerning the 1971-72 state urban education allocations. This letter stated that "Parent-Community involvement in the planning of reimbursable programs is basic to their success" and advised that the Board of

Education require a public hearing on all urban education programs prior to their submission. A certification form signed by the school board chairman and community superintendent was required to be affixed to each proposal before submission.

The results of the revised legislation and Scribner's policy guidelines created an environment that allowed CSB District 3 in Manhattan to sue the Board of Education successfully to have all 31 school boards control the reimbursable funds. In essence, the resulting decision gave parents and residents in each district virtual control over these funds. However, as already indicated, change-agent districts proceeded to create advisory bodies consonant with the law. In those cases—all too many—where the CSB's are status quo oriented, they guard their power so jealously that, even though they formed advisory bodies, they continue to conduct business as usual. On those school boards (23, 14, and 16) where Title I allocations are in the millions, one would expect that, in the light of the low achievement levels of minority pupils, credited in part to an unresponsive bureaucracy, community school boards as "true representatives" of the people would welcome all opportunities to involve their constituents. The activities of many boards dampened such hopes.

PROFILE OF THE BOARDS

Of the 31 community school boards in New York City, 23 are status quo, 6 are active, and 2 are change agent.

Both change-agent boards (3 and 13) are in districts that are predominantly black or Puerto Rican. Similarly, all 6 (2, 4, 7, 10, 12, and 17) of the minimally active school boards are in districts where the student population of blacks and Puerto Ricans is above 60 percent. Of the remaining 23 school boards, all of which are status quo, 12 of them (1, 5, 6, 8, 9, 14, 15, 16, 19, 23, 28, and 29) are in districts that are predominantly black. The remaining 11 school boards (11, 18, 20, 21, 22, 24, 25, 26, 27, 30, and 31) are in districts where the white student population ranges from 66 percent to as high as 89 percent (CSB 22). Significantly, not a single board in the white districts experienced a high degree of prolonged conflict.

Change-Agent Boards

Of the two districts with change-agent boards, District 3 has a pupil population distribution that is 31 percent Puerto Rican, 50

TABLE 14

Change-Agent Boards

CSB	Racial Composition of CSB				Pupil Population				New District Superintendent Hired	
	PR	B	W	O	PR	B	W	O	Yes	Race
3	2	2	4		31	50	18		X	PR
13	1	5	3		22	73	5		X	B

percent black, and 18 percent white; District 13's pupil population ratio is 22 percent Puerto Rican, 73 percent black, and 5 percent white.

Both boards appointed new superintendents when they took office. CSB 3 chose the first Puerto Rican superintendent, and CSB 13 appointed a black superintendent.

Apart from the appointment of new black and Puerto Rican district superintendents, the two boards are characterized by impressive innovation in the policy areas, of budget, curriculum, personnel, and frequent ratification of parents' choices of principals. In addition, they both made extra effort to involve parents and residents as partners in the making of educational policy.

CSB 3

CSB 3 appointed Alfredo Mathew as its community superintendent. Interviews with school board members gave him high ratings for his performance. Community residents, too, praised his leadership. At public meetings his expertise is frequently consulted and relied upon. His refusal to report the reading scores of the Spanish-speaking pupils to the central Board endeared him to both the community and the school board. The CSB, with general community approval, extended his contract for another year.

As one of the most "progressive" districts in the city, CSB 3 has fought against central constraints in at least three cases. It has used the law as a weapon for effecting change and has accepted the responsibility for a major role in developing school policy for its schools. It sued the city Board to compel compliance with federal and state laws concerning distribution of federal and state funds and won. It sued the central Board and Chancellor for violating the education law in failing to perform its budgetary duties and lost the case. It also sued the Board over that body's excessing rules, which stipulated that substitutes must be dropped before tenured teachers. It lost this case.

		Innovativeness		
		Personnel (principals hired off lists)	Frequency of CBS's Ratification of Parents' Choice of Principal	Extra Effort made to Involve Parents
Budget	Curriculum			
X	X	13	13/13	X
X	X	11	11/11	X

It is significant that CSB 3 has used litigation as a main thrust in its fight with the central Board. The ambiguous laws are viewed as offering an important means of increasing local board powers.

In District 3, parents are involved in screening principals; their recommendations have consistently been respected. On budget and curriculum, Title I funds are overwhelmingly allocated on a local option basis. These programs are designed and developed by the school's Funded Programs Committee and parents. Local option programs must be approved by the CSB and the district superintendent. Moreover, the CSB sees to it that programs under Title I conform to federal guidelines and are reasonably designed to meet the needs of all eligible Title I children.

In an effort to involve the community further and meet the service needs of the district's schools, the CSB had established a field office in Harlem. Because of budget cuts and increases in costs of operation, the CSB in January 1972 voted to close that office and seek out alternative methods of servicing that community. CSB members interviewed indicated that they welcomed the opportunity to hear community views. Parents are given time to present their position when a matter is under consideration. Board members emphasize, however, that more contact with the community exists prior to public meetings—in special meetings with PA's, in the schools, etc. Of course, business must be transacted in public meetings.

Board 3 sought alternative ways to achieve its objective of educational advancement. This a worthwhile measurement of a board's orientation to its task. Vigorous community participation and the search for alternative ways brought about phenomenal changes in principalships and in the distribution of funds allocated for compensatory programs and an increase in the number of pedagogical employees whose services were terminated.

In its first year of operation, CSB 3 refused to give tenure to two principals; four probationary teachers were also terminated. In appointments made possible under the Mansfield injunction, the district has hired 13 black and Puerto Rican principals not on the Board of Examiners' lists. The only other district that comes close to this record is CSB district 13, which appointed blacks and Puerto Ricans to 9 of its 11 principal vacancies. About one-half of the district's Title I funds went for SEC, none for MES, and about one-tenth for the 5P program, another UFT-sponsored program.

CSB 13

CSB 13 appointed Stanley Taylor, a black, as its community superintendent. His is a personality that elicits strong emotions of love and hate. One board member, asked what was his greatest satisfaction from serving on the CSB, replied, "My voting for Stanley Taylor as district superintendent."[9] Another CSB member said that his resignation as board chairman was due to the hostility he feels for Taylor. It has also been reported that the community itself was split over his appointment, but even the losing faction and its leaders have since been silenced by the effective leadership Taylor displays. The community superintendent's major accomplishment has been his ability to unite and lead the district. In keeping with his image as leader and chief administrator of the district, the superintendent does not dominate the board. At public meetings, he does not try to manipulate questioners or dodge the questions; his replies are forthright and sincere.

The CSB has created mechanisms to facilitate the involvement of parents in the decision-making process, and the parents are actively taking advantage of these arrangements. In matters relating to the selection of principals or teachers or in matters concerning the development of curriculum or the expenditure of funds to a school, the PA's and PTA's become the fulcrum in the decision-making process. The board's rationale is that, since the decisions relate to a specific school and affect a specific segment of the district's community, it is essential that appropriate representatives of this community be the moving forces in deciding such matters. For example, when two acting assistant principalships (at PS 20 and PS 54) and one acting principalship, Rothschild Junior High School (294), were to be filled, screening committees composed of PA and PTA members and individual parents from those schools were established. In using this procedure the CSB brought decentralization to the individual school level. In cases of conflict between community-based organizations and a school's community, this provision works to the benefit of those who would be most affected by the decision—the individual school's constituency. In all three instances of choosing principals, the CSB met in executive session, interviewed the individuals, and voted in favor of the recommendation of both the parents' and the community's organizations.

In matters of a more general nature affecting the district as a whole, members of groups that are organized in the community (community corporations and community planning boards) plus representatives from Parents' Associations and Parents' Associations Councils have the strongest voice. For example, the involvement of parents in the evaluation of Title I programs in the district came as a direct result of pressure exercised by these organized groups on the CSB. The CSB, desirous of keeping the peace, sold the idea of parent involvement to the Institute for Educational Development (IED) evaluators. In 1971 alone, over 1,000 parents benefited from this experience. They were allowed to enter teachers' classrooms without prior notice and to observe them during the process of instruction. Though, at first, some teachers (both black and white) resented non-professionals reviewing them, as the project progressed the teachers welcomed them. They came to realize that the parents' interests in the school resulted from genuine concern for their children's future rather than from political ambitions or the desire to "get Whitey."

Each CSB member is accountable to the CSB for a knowledge of what happens in each school. To carry out this duty, the CSB member meets with PA and PTA members, individually and organizationally, informally and officially. They apprise him of their problems and suggest solutions to him.

CSB 13 has developed significant measures that have minimized the high rate of pupil and teacher absenteeism. Because the formula for the allocation of tax-levy funds is based on average daily attendance of pupils, by increasing the number of students attending school daily, the CSB made a net gain of tens of thousands of dollars. Also, because the number of substitute teachers was drastically reduced, the district made another substantial saving. Furthermore, the introduction of a planning-programming-budgeting system (PPBS) eliminated some excess items from the budget and resulted in more savings.

In curriculum, the PA's and PTA's stand in the forefront of innovative changes in the district. In one school, PS 307, three community persons spearheaded opposition to continuing the MES program there. Now, this program exists only in a modified form. The PTA at PS 67 eliminated the Experimental Elementary Program and in its stead created a Diagnostic Reading Center. CSB 13 also created a Reading Diagnostic Clinic, whose purpose is to diagnose the areas of weakness of those children who read below grade level so that a reading program can be tailored to their individual needs.

CSB 13 has hired 11 black principals since it took office. The CSB's administrative staff at 44 Court Street is almost 90 percent black. This is a positive note in view of the fact that the district is about 80 percent black and Puerto Rican. Also, it is felt that the presence of minority administration walking through the schools helps to create a positive image of identity for black and Puerto Rican students.

CSB 13, in spite of the statutory restrictions of time, has recruited and appointed a significant number of minority teachers through the alternate-hiring system. The CSB combined teacher recruitment as an integral aspect of its Title I program, the Student Interne Cooperative Education Program. "Under this program," reports the Community School System Law Letter, "50 student teachers from Southern and Puerto Rican colleges have been recruited to undertake their senior year of student teaching assignments in schools of the district."[10] At the expiration of their internship, those who are qualified are appointed as teachers beginning the following September.

Education assistants (EA's) are now being trained in conjunction with teachers. This type of in-service training aims at developing some sort of coordination and esprit de corps between teacher and education assistant. Parents had complained that in great number of instances the teacher, either through ignorance or malice, used the EA as a lackey. A second area of in-service training concentrates on using high school students to bolster the small complement of EA's. This service is most helpful in individualized reading programs where one teacher and two EA's are insufficient.

Active Boards

We have classified six boards as active: CSB's 2, 4, 7, 10, 12, and 17. The major difference between them and change-agent boards is that, although they have involved the community in some ways, they do not view their role as fundamental to change in the educational system.

CSB 2

This CSB, at one of its first meetings, hired Dr. Elliott Shapiro as its district superintendent. Shapiro enjoyed the reputation of being a tough-minded and innovative principal in a Harlem School. Several persons, board members and community residents alike, spoke favorably of him. An observer at the public meeting at which he was appointed equated the scene to that of a National Presidential Convention; there were placards with favorable inscriptions and the name of the district's section displaying them. Shapiro's supporters

even carried him on their shoulders as they marched around the
auditorium, triumphant in their hour of victory.

His relationship with the school board was amiable, cordial,
and respectful. On taking office he made it clear that he considered
his appointment acceptance of his role as educational expert and
chief administrator of the district. This determination resulted in
uneasiness on a number of occasions. First, he sought to establish
that members of the district staff could not be assigned work by the
CSB members. When the CSB decided to initiate monthly meetings
with the principal, he opposed the idea on the ground that such an
action would undermine his authority vis-à-vis the principals. Also
when community residents objected to the appointments of a deputy
superintendent and a community relations specialist without prior
advertisement or community consultation, Shapiro made the vote on
this issue a vote of confidence for himself. Arrogantly he declaimed,
"The district would collapse unless the motion to appoint these two
assistants were successfully passed tonight." The motion was carried.

On the three occasions noted, the CSB and the community were
reluctant to confront their chief administrator for fear of polarizing
the community or fragmenting the coalition of whites, blacks, and
Puerto Ricans who together have fought for the development of professional accountability in the district.

His resignation came as relief to growing opposition groups.
As his disenchantment grew with an increasing inability to repeat the
great feats that he had accomplished under the old system in Harlem,
so, too, the CSB became more intolerant of his petty demands.

After his resignation, procedures were put in motion to select
a new community superintendent. Representatives of the PA's took
part in the interviews. The deputy superintendent was chosen to
replace Shaprio as superintendent.

CSB 2 was one of the boards most affected by the budget cuts;
nearly 200 teaching and guidance positions were lost. In a different
budget area, CSB 2 did attempt to achieve a major accomplishment.
The district decided to convert the kitchens of five schools, which had
served soup-and-sandwich lunches, to prepackaged frozen-food lunches.
Central headquarters estimated the cost was $100,000 to $250,000 per
school with the conversion to take two to three years. Appalled at
such a ridiculously high estimate, the school board contacted private
food preparation concerns which provided technical assistance as
part of their service. Limiting the conversions to essential ovens
and freezers, CSB 2 was able to convert the kitchens to frozen-food
lunches provided by the private contractor at $3,000-$5,000 per
school. This represents a saving of from $475,000 to $1.22 million.
The central board of Education enjoined the CSB from discharging its

contract with the food concern. CSB 2 then sued the city Board for
blocking its efforts to operate its own lunch program and won in a
decision that will ease the way of the other CSB's desirous of handling
their own food services.

The CSB also allocated its funds so that it was able to set up an
after-school reading program. This move, like the food service decisions, indicate that the CSB did not react passively to budget matters
as did so many community school boards.

Since its inception CSB 2 has appointed six acting principals,
two acting assistant principals, and three assistant principals. The
CSB has indicated a desire to employ teachers of minority backgrounds.
The past board chairman stated the board's eagerness to adopt the
alternative method of hiring in those schools that qualify and where
vacancies occur. The CSB also approved in In-Migrant.Program,
which includes on-the-job training leading to a teaching license for
Spanish-speaking persons who have taught elsewhere—primarily in
Puerto Rico—but do not meet New York City licensing requirements.
Thirteen such teachers have been interviewed and approved, but
stringent budgetary measures made hiring impossible.

CSB 2 has developed two innovative education programs. One
is an experimental school in PS 3. This program caters to children
from kindergarten to sixth grade and operates on an open-classroom
basis. The student population of the school is somewhat over 300. The
teachers all have teachers' licenses issued by the Board of Education,
but they are specially chosen for this school by the parents.

The other program of which the district is particularly proud
is the Clinton Program, referred to as a school without walls, whose
campus is the city. The children are taken frequently to different
city businesses, industries, and government offices, exposing them
firsthand to the actual day-to-day operations of these enterprises.

CSB 4

This district basically includes the East Harlem community.
Its school population is 65 percent Puerto Rican, 33 percent black,
and 2 percent white. In spite of a black-Puerto Rican conflict, the
CSB's performance has often been impressive.

Consistent with legal requirements, the by-laws of this CSB
give the parents a considerable voice in the hiring of supervisors. The
final choice is by the CSB, but that choice must be made from those
names the parents' groups have recommended. In hiring an architect
for drawing up the design and plan for the new PS 74, the CSB insisted
that the firm consult the PA and emphasized that it was the PA's
right to determine what should be in this building and that the architect
should respect their judgment at all times.

Specially funded programs are handled on a local option basis where each PA has a considerable input with respect to the programs affecting its schools. Expectedly, bilingual programs are emphasized. This certainly was not the case prior to decentralization.

This district has refused to be subservient to the mandates of the central Board of Education. It challenged the constitutionality of the UFT's excessing provisions because they result in de facto discrimination; it has denied tenure in four cases. It has recently appointed the youngest school board member in the state, thus challenging the age limit set in the legislation, and the New York State Attorney General has validated this action.

This active community involvement resulted in the appointment of five minority principals (four Puerto Ricans and one black) where none had existed before and the development of a massive bilingual program because of the board's recognition of the utility of this program as a learning device for non-English-speaking pupils. In short, the aggressive posture of this CSB with respect to educational matters imbues the board as an agent of change.

CSB 7

CSB 7 services the South Bronx community. This district has the lowest achievement levels of the Bronx districts, perhaps the lowest in the city.

Upon assuming office, the school board rehired the incumbent superintendent. Subsequent events highlighted some difficulties with that decision. Community involvement was limited and tensions developed between blacks and Puerto Ricans. The community superintendent was frequently absent from public meetings, and when he did attend meetings he remained silent. Effective May 1, 1972, he resigned his post.

At present the board is composed of two blacks, two Puerto Ricans, and five whites. With 66 percent of the student population Puerto Rican, 32 percent black, and only 2 percent white, the school board is racially unrepresentative of both the larger community and the school population.

Probably because of this fact, the CSB has an erratic commitment to community participation. The CSB passed a resolution that demands that personnel hired in District 7 schools must have the consent of the board member attached to that school. The board's rationale was that this provision would "provide positive control of the staffing of the district and would clarify the procedure when personnel are recommended for employment."[11]

Parents are consulted in the selection of sites for schools, but so too are teachers and principals. Public hearings are also held.

The CSB created its Title I advisory committee in accordance with law, and the majority of voting members are parents. There are 23 parents—1 from each school, 4 community agency representatives, 1 principal, 1 UFT representative, 4 nonpublic school representatives. Despite this, however, program proposals are still heavily influenced by the professional staff of the district. Notices of public meetings are circulated well in advance in both English and Spanish. They are usually short, containing only a numerical notation of the agenda items, with no explanations of resolutions. Despite the CSB's seeming responsive attitude to the community, there are serious shortcomings that attend the board.

On two occasions in the 1971-72 school year, open public meetings were canceled. On the latter occasion, 300 residents of the community were disappointed when the public meeting was rescheduled because of the lack of a quorum. Only five members were present. Great public attention had been focused on this meeting because much debate was expected on two of the agenda items: the confirmation of a coordinator for project redesign, and the appointment of three assistant principals. Both of these items demanded the urgent attention of the board because the appointed personnel could not assume their duties until the decisions of an executive meeting were voted upon at an open public meeting.

Another time, the chairperson of the Quality Incentive Program (QIP) advisory committee expressed dissatisfaction with the CSB's handling of some QIP monies. Deriding the board for allocating these funds to pay the salaries of five guidance assistants, the chairperson remarked, "There is some confusion about how the additional guidance assistants would be utilized. We believe the CSB owes us an explanation."[12]

There have been personality struggles on the board among the Puerto Rican faction, and some board members view these as the major reason for inaction and the limited role the board has played in seeking change. Expectedly, these personality conflicts spill over into the larger community. For instance, the PTA of PS 161 has a Puerto Rican leadership while the PTA of PS 162 has a black leadership, and each of these parent groups has its spokesmen on the CSB. The consequence of this is that the CSB experiences great frustration in resolving issues because each board member tends to articulate the views of the clique he represents. A further consequence is that these ethnic tensions between blacks and Puerto Ricans imperil the smooth functioning of the board. Meetings seldom begin on time. Sometimes meetings are postponed because of the lack of a quorum. For a couple of months, the CSB scheduled all its meetings for the afternoon. The intent of this move was to limit the number of community youth and parents, who, it was thought, disrupted the meetings. Though the

afternoon meetings curtailed incidents of disruption, one of the un-
intended consequences was limited communication resulting in limited
participation at a time when cooperation was most needed. This need
was underscored by Carmen Martinez upon her resignation as chairperson of the board. She said,

> There is a lack of communication between the community
> and some CSB members. We cannot have effective com-
> munity control while these gaps exist. . . . Board members
> have a moral obligation to consult parents in their schools
> before making decisions. This includes attending as many
> PA meetings as possible and keeping parents informed on
> a regular basis.[13]

Several board members complain about union and central Board
constraints as more important reasons for their limited role. Activist
community groups have pressured for an increased role for parents,
but the CSB has responded in a restrained manner.

There has been a plethora of curriculum programs in this
district since decentralization. Private industry is involved in many
of the new programs. Equitable Life Insurance, Western Electric,
Chemical Bank, Sachs New York, Pfizer, and the Port Authority
worked out relationships with some schools in the district. Under this
project, called BOAT (Better Occupational Awareness Training),
selected classes, parents, and staff frequented these places of business
so as to acquaint the children with the daily operation of large industries and enterprises, not to mention the opportunities for employment
that they offer.

Other programs include a newspaper club in every JHS. This
program was formulated in the belief that students learn best when
they are doing things that are practical and meaningful to them. The
Math Labs in all 23 elementary schools in the district provide small
group instruction and use a variety of concrete materials that many
claim facilitate the imparting of knowledge. The joint program of
bilingualism and Puerto Rican history and culture is taught to the
third, fourth, and fifth grades in the elementary schools and to the
seventh and eighth grades in the junior high schools. Seventy-three
teachers assisted by as many paraprofessionals instruct the students
in this program. The special primary school at PS 31 combines the
best features of the MES and the All-Day Neighborhood School concepts. Furthermore, an overlay of instructional and supportive
staff reduce teacher-pupil ratio. An after-school study center is
also provided, involving remediation in reading and math as well as
cultural enrichment. Also, a budget officer has been hired.

In personnel, the school board has hired over 15 principals,
many of them black and Puerto Rican and many of them not on the

lists. They are now interviewing candidates for community superintendent and it is likely that a Puerto Rican will be appointed to that
position. There is also a paraprofessional development course that
provides intensive training in the teaching of basic reading and
mathematical skills; 130 paraprofessionals were undergoing this
training.

CSB 10

 CSB 10 includes the Riverdale, Fordham, and Tremont areas in
the Bronx. It is an integrated district and the student population is
22 percent Puerto Rican, 21 percent black, and 57 percent white.
With a school board composed of one Puerto Rican and eight whites,
the unrepresentative nature of the school board is at once evident.
 Despite this imbalance in the board's composition, racial and
ethnic conflict is minimal, due probably to the low activity of minority
groups. The little tension that exists is between white middle-class
parents and the white-dominated school board.
 In an article on December 25, 1970, Fox Butterfield, a New
York Times reporter, effusively praised CSB 10. He noted that "7
principals and 9 assistant principals were appointed by the school
board after it consulted with the parents association of the schools
involved and allowed the parents' groups to take part in the meetings
at which the candidates were interviewed."[14] Unfortunately, the
board's own minutes plus interviews with board members and residents of the community failed to corroborate Butterfield's account
of the board's consistent involvement of parents in key areas of decision-making.
 The community school board involves parents and residents in
only peripheral areas of policy-making. Though it worked out formal
ways for effectuating this involvement, in the critical areas of personnel selection and the granting of tenure, neither parents nor other
community residents have a significant input. For example, the
school board grants tenure to employees, afterward notifying the PA's
of its action. A CSB memorandum is illustrative in this regard.
The notification to the PA reads, in part,

 This will serve to notify you publicly that the Community
 School Board of School District 10 of the New York City
 Board of Education has granted tenure in the district to
 the following supervisory personnel who have been appointed by this Board in accordance with the provisions
 of the Education Law of 1969 as amended by A7427/S6291:
 . . .[15]

Then follow the names of the candidates, their file numbers, their dates of appointment, and the school to which each is attached.

A further illustration of the board's attitude to parental involvement was underscored by Isobel Rooney, a member of the school board. She scored the board's personnel procedure regarding the granting of tenure as being "highly irregular." Furthermore, she questioned the criteria the CSB used in preparing the lists for the various schools and said:

> I was at a loss to understand this action since the agenda of that meeting was not furnished to me beforehand, and especially since the action was not taken at a public meeting where the community would have an opportunity to express its views. You will note that the item of tenure was not included on the agenda as distributed for this public meeting, and I asked that it be added.
>
> The persons named on the supervisors' tenure list had not completed their probationary periods or anywhere near it. The Parents' Associations were not consulted regarding the granting of tenure by the Board until after the executive meeting where the attempt was made to grant tenure. The granting of tenure was publicized as official before it was presented at a public meeting.[16]

On another issue, the CSB was accused of duplicity in excluding from the agenda of the March 1971 public meeting the second extension of the community superintendent's leave of absence, though the board knew full well that the item would be dealt with. This procedure undermined the ability of the community to arrive at its position clearly on such an important matter. Secondly, it was thought that the CSB forced the issue and extended the superintendent's leave of absence to September because the short time lapse would enable the CSB to choose the candidate of their choice "without much interference from the community."[17]

The procedure to fill the superintendency began with advertisements in two New York newspapers on June 13 and 20, 1971 announcing the vacancy and soliciting applications. Parents were present at the screening and selection of the 45 candidates; they had access to the candidates' résumés but could not vote on the candidates. Also present at the interviews were representatives of the professional and supervisory staffs of the district. The larger community was not represented at the screening and selection because according to Dr. Robert Christen, a CSB member, "members of the CSB were elected for the purpose of representing the entire community." Another board member reasoned that

according to the Community School Board mailing list
there are some 300 community groups in our district who
were eligible to participate under the title of "community
groups." To facilitate and expedite the process of interviewing candidates for Community Superintendent, the
Board decided to invite the parents of the schools involved.[18]

Though the CSB has no district newspaper and though weekly
executive meetings are closed to the public, the CSB keeps the community well informed by several new mechanisms and formal procedures. Notices of public meetings are sent out well in advance, accompanied with an itemized agenda. The minutes of public meetings
are very detailed and are available to any one who wants them. At
times however, the minutes were substantially challenged by parents.
One parent accused the board of willfully and maliciously deleting
from the minutes events that took place because they were damaging
to the board. Another parent accused the board of distorting events to
cast the board in a better light than it deserves.
    Upon assuming office, CSB 10 hired a new community super-
intendent. He was appointed in July 1970 but did not begin to discharge
his duties until shortly before the beginning of the 1971-72 school
year due to vacation and his presence at a symposium on the West
Coast. In November 1970 he requested and received a leave of absence
on account of illness. In the spring of 1971 he again requested and
was granted extended sick leave to September 1971. Though the act
of choosing a new community superintendent reflects the dedication
of the school board to "meet the education needs of the disadvantaged
as well as the gifted child, not to mention a large number of children
that fall in between" and though the candidate chosen was a man of
unquestioned ability, there has been a considerable amount of negative
comment on his superintendency.[19]
    Pierre Marique Jr., a consultant to the Neighborhood Council
of Young People of Greater New York, criticized the community
superintendent for his repeated requests for extended leave and
warned him that "the granting of these extensions . . . casts a very
definite cloud over your reputation for straightforwardness."[20]
    Though the CSB does not involve the community directly in
decision-making and though the formal procedures set up for achieving
participation fall far short of their stated goals, the CSB has indicated
a willingness to change. The CSB worked out a roll-call procedure
with the PA's, whereby each school in the district presents its views
on agenda items. At a public meeting in May 1971 the board adopted
a resolution to place copies of its by-laws in every public library in the
district. According to board members, this would allow the community
to become more thoroughly acquainted with the board's actions.

As of March 22, 1971, the CSB decided to tape the proceedings of all public meetings and keep the tape in the district office for three months, during which time residents of the district are free to review them.

Regarding public hearings, the CSB sees its role as an "arbiter not as a party to a dispute." To this end, it worked out formal procedures for the conduct of public hearings similar to procedures adopted by the Board of Estimate and the Site Selection Board.[21] In brief, the CSB opens the floor to speakers with negative depositions; proponents of the issue speak next; at the end of the testimony, the chairman calls for a motion to close the hearing; then the CSB exercises one of three options: approve, disapprove, or table the motion for a future date. Expectedly, then, the CSB has some few minimal changes to show for its efforts. Regarding budget, representatives of the CSB visited a commercial lunch program in some schools in North Bergen, New Jersey. Secondly, by forcing the Board of Education to comply with CSB 10's decision to use capital funds for repairs, the CSB saved thousands of dollars. As to personnel, few persons have been hired who are not on the lists. No inroads were made to the basic curriculum. A program consisting of the best curriculum programs in the district and known as the Institute on Individualized Instruction was developed. Teachers and supervisors in the district were requested to attend the institute on one of four evenings as part of the teacher-training program.

The district's summer Title I program would service almost 15 percent of its school population (3,876) as follows:

Program	Number of Pupils Participating
Head Start	400
Extended School Program	1,160
ENRICH	216
VISIT	300
STAI	900
Belmont Association	900
Total	3,876

CSB 12

CSB district 12 encompasses the communities of Morrisania, the southern tip of Morris Park, and the southern tip of Tremont. Only 7.2 percent of the eligible voters elected a racially unrepresentative CSB of six whites, one black, and two Puerto Ricans.

The CSB is basically oriented to involving parents in the creation of school policy. It has spelled out procedures and has taken the position that parents are responsible for their individual schools, while general policy-making for the district is reserved for the school board. Had there been serious splits between the CSB and the community, the board's proposal for a division of labor would have redounded to the disadvantage of the community. On the contrary, parental involvement in personnel selection is good. Parents are engaged in the initial screening and are present at final interviews. Though the CSB exercises its legal right to have the final say, it is to the credit of the board that in very many instances the parents' choice of principals is coterminous with that of the board's.

Upon assuming office CSB 12 appointed Dr. Edythe Gaines, a black school professional, as its first community superintendent. During her years in the district as teacher and principal she fought for the educational benefit of minority pupils through the establishment of a variety of new programs. Upon her resignation to become head of the chancellor's Learning Cooperative in 1972 the school board selected Dr. Felton Lewis, also a black, to succeed her. He is of an independent mind and seeks to exert his influence and knowledge at all times, but always with the achievement of the pupils of the district as his top priority.

CSB 12 has hired seven minority principals. At present, the CSB has put together a team to go to Puerto Rico and the South to recruit persons as teachers and principals. At a time of budget cutbacks in education and rising unemployment throughout the nation, CSB 12 has hired 1,000 paraprofessionals, many of whom are enrolled in college programs.

CSB 12 boasts many innovative programs, including the Pupil-Personnel Team, which entails the coordinated effort of several schools in the district in utilizing and sharing their technical personnel. It is like a task force that is shifted about to suit area and need. Another innovation is the Integrated Curriculum Program of Math and Science, in which math and science are taught as one subject rather than separately. The aim here is probably to prove the common assertion that mathematics is the language of science. For children, then, who fear science but are at home with math, or vice versa, this program has proven to be of incalculable benefit. In additions, PS 77 and PS 92 are experimenting with the open-classroom method of teaching. At PS 97 and PS 129, Dr. Caleb Gattegno, mentioned earlier, is attempting to put his dictum "If you know a little, you know a lot" into practice. Each of these schools, though physically joined together, has its own principal, assistant principal, and complement of teachers.

No final evaluation has yet been made of these programs, and such an evaluation is eagerly awaited.

CSB 17

CSB 17 chose as its community superintendent a white, Dr. Charles I. Schonhaut. His success over the first two years of decentralization resulted in a renewal of his contract for another three-year term. In a time of conflict between groups on many issues, it was unusual to hear so very many black parents fervently praise a white superintendent for his accomplishments.

In CSB 17 the key to decision-making is the Education Advisory Council, comprised of parents, one representative from each of the indigenous district organizations, one representative from the parochial schools, plus any CSB member who wishes to attend. The 1972 summer Title I programs were created on the basis of just such a parent evaluation of the 1971 summer program.

The involvement of the Education Advisory Council by the community school board resulted in the creation of an innovative program, the Flatbush Extension Program. This is a school unit whose educational orientation is similar to that of a 600 school, for the socially maladjusted. There is one assistant principal, one reading specialist, one math teacher, and two educational assistants. At present, the unit has a population of 20 boys chosen from among the "intractables" of the district's junior high schools. Because of the individual disciplinary problems these boys posed in their schools, the teachers at Flatbush Extension accompany them to lunch and maintain a close communication link with the boys' parents.

The CSB has engaged the Institute for Educational Development to evaluate the program, with the help of community residents and organizations. The reason for the early evaluation given by Eleanor Pittman, one of the two Title I coordinators, is to allow parents and the CSB to compare the significance of both the MES and the SEC programs, two centrally mandated programs that cost about $1 million each.

In principal replacement selection, four of the seven vacancies that occurred during the board's tenure were filled by blacks. In one case, parents induced one of the candidates to leave his position at central headquarters for a principalship in the district. The parents claimed that when he worked in the district as an assistant principal he did an outstanding job.

Status Quo Community School Boards in
Minority Districts

Status quo school boards can be subdivided into two categories: those in minority districts and those in white districts. The boards are all in districts (1, 5, 6, 8, 9, 14, 15, 16, 19, 23, 28, and 29 where both the student population and the larger community are ethnically homogenous—black and/or Puerto Rican. These boards can be further divided into two subtypes: those where the CSB's are unrepresentative (that is, white-dominated): 8, 15, 16, and 19; and those torn by conflict: 1, 5, 6, 9, 14, 23, 28, and 29.

Status Quo: Unrepresentative

CSB 8

    CSB 8 services, in the main, the East Central Bronx, including the communities of East Tremont, West Farms, Morrisania, Classon Point, Hunts Point, and Throgs Neck. Of the eligible voters, 13.5 percent went to the polls during the school board elections of 1969 and elected a school board composed of one black and eight whites. In a district whose student population is 42 percent Puerto Rican, 30 percent black, and 28 percent white, the CSB is clearly unrepresentative, a fact not mitigated by the addition of two Puerto Rican members, who replaced two whites who had resigned.

    This situation has caused some problems for the district. CSB-community tension has arisen because of the board's unwillingness to involve the community in its decision-making process. The CSB lacks reliable reporting. Notices of public meetings are sent out sporadically, agendas are supplied infrequently, and minutes of public meetings are difficult to obtain, and, at times, they just do not exist. This difficulty of obtaining minutes reflects both the board's incompetence and its paternalistic attitude.

    The community is frustrated by the board. Several examples will illustrate this point. A vacancy on the school board existed for at least six months with no community resident applying for the position. In March, 1972, a well-known community activist fought against the candidacy of a more traditional-minded person for a school board vacancy and lost. On another matter, the community became so incensed with the CSB that the public meetings ended in a near riot.

    If school reformers are right that a board's choice of its community superintendent is a significant index of its potential for success, then CSB 8 got off to a bad start by rehiring the incumbent superintendent. When he resigned, the school board was given a second opportunity to choose a competent administrator. After one year spokesmen for the CSB said they were disenchanted with their new chief administrator. They confided that they "were looking for a man with a firm hand who could make decisions. We got just the opposite."[22] Though the CSB's disenchantment with its new community superintendent can be understood, it remains an irrefutable testimony to the

CSB's evaluation of prospective personnel and, in a larger sense, to its ability to function competently.

In a district fraught with problems of overcrowding, high teacher turnover, and underachievement in reading and mathematics, one would expect the CSB and the community superintendent to be active in curriculum development, curriculum change and so on, and to be asserting their position on issues and adopting policy for the district. The community superintendent refrains from this. On the contrary, his reports at public meetings are always exhortatory. Things are going to improve. The CSB neither challenges the superintendent nor initiates efforts of its own.

This status quo board did not alter basic curriculum. PS 39 has an open-classroom component, and a prekindergarten program was established in PS 48, the first in the district. With all of its 27 schools (23 PS's and 4 JHS's) Title I schools, most of the reimbursable funds still go the centrally mandated MES and SEC programs.

A business manager has been hired, and about three principals were hired who were not on the lists.

CSB 15

CSB 15 covers the South Brooklyn and parts of the Park Slope communities in Brooklyn. The school board is composed of nine white members in a district where the pupil distribution is 49 percent Puerto Rican, 17 percent black, and 34 percent white.

To a limited extent, the CSB involves the community in its deliberations. For instance, nine vacancies for principalships were filled by the school board, and in eight of those nine cases the CSB ratified the parents' selection. However, when it came to creating a team to evaluate the district's entire curriculum program, the CSB chose six professionals, and although three PTA representatives dissented from the substance of the final report, the CSB adopted the report without even considering the dissenting opinions. Expectedly, the substance of the dissent dealt with restructuring the basic curriculum.

The CSB stands adamant against parental visits to the classrooms of their children. In addition, no effort has been made to hire personnel not on the eligibility lists. Though two teachers were dismissed (one for assaulting a child and the other for excessive lateness), the CSB generally grants tenure to teachers and principals automatically.

CSB 16

CSB 16 includes parts of the communities of Bushwick-Ridgewood, Bedford-Stuyvesant, Crown Heights, and Williamsburg. Of its eligible residents, 8 percent participated in the 1969 school elections. They elected two whites, two Puerto Ricans, and five blacks to the school board.

This school board does not involve the community in school policy-making. The appointment of supervisory personnel is one area in which conflict has arisen between the school board and the community. The result is that very little is accomplished and the contempt of the community for the board has grown substantially. For example, the issue of granting tenure to an acting principal who came up for tenure in October 1971 grew into an issue that engaged the board for three months not solely because of the community's opposition to the candidate but also because of what parents consider the board's policy of acting without their knowledge.

At the December 1971 public meeting, parents complained of the late arrival of notices for public meetings. To date, the CSB has taken no real action to remedy this situation. Spanish-speaking parents requested that the notices of public meetings be written bilingually. Remedy in this area too has been slow in coming.

Notice of public meetings are mailed five days in advance to only those persons whose names appear on a mailing list. In addition, even though the CSB's by-laws call for them, detailed agendas for public meetings have not been provided by the board. Furthermore, according to the CSB's by-laws, public meetings ought to be rotated between JHS 26, JHS 35, JHS 111, and PS 299. In contravention of its own ruling and with little consideration for the feelings of the community, the CSB holds its meetings only at JHS 26.

Executive meetings are held biweekly and are closed to the public. In contrast, the two change-agent boards (3 and 13) hold executive meetings on a weekly basis and make them open to parents and residents. The openness of executive school board meetings, apart from giving the community a firsthand look at its elected school representatives in the act of making policy, provides a link in communication that the decentralization law itself did not provide. In addition, CSB 16 held no public meetings in November 1971, and the December 1971 meeting had no quorum.

All of the 27 schools (23 PS's and 4 JHS's) in the district are Title I schools. This situation is indicative of consistently low scores on the Metropolitan Achievement Test. Though the superintendent was part of the old system and as such was partially responsible for the educational deterioration, the new school board rehired the old superintendent. The expected consequence is that, rather than pushing the board to be responsive to the demands of the community, he acts a buffer between the CSB and the community, which reinforces the do-nothingness of the board.

At public meetings, the superintendent has the dominant role. Questions are directed to him and he answers them unhesitatingly.

Parents are often not given appropriate answers when they seek to know such simple things as the requirements for Intellectually Gifted Children classes or the entrance procedures and requirements for specialized high schools like Brooklyn Technical or Hunter.

Due to the absence of strong indigenous organizations, the influence of the school systems is all pervasive. Almost 75 percent of the audience at public meetings are from the staff of the district's schools. The CSB's dealings with the unions are ones of extreme caution and strict interpretation of the contract. One CSB member reminded an interviewer that "we <u>must</u> follow exactly what the contract calls for."

This attitude of the CSB, characteristic of that dictum, permeates the CSB's educational policy. With no parental participation and strict adherence to emasculating central Board's guidelines, curriculum and budget innovation have been negligible and deviation from old-line personnel practices has been infrequent.

No change has taken place either in the basic curriculum or in Title I programs. For Title I, the board has maintained all the centrally mandated programs: MES, SEC, District School for Children with Learning Difficulties, Auxiliary Training Programs, and College Prep.

Except for the appointment of a business manager, salaried at $18,000 per annum, this CSB has done nothing in the area of budget. Traditional hiring procedures have been maintained with strong reliance on the central Board staff and regulations. There are few signs of change in the district.

Status Quo: High-Conflict School Boards

These boards fall into two subcategories. Those in which there is an overrepresentation of whites—1, 6, 9, 14, 28, and 29—and those that are completely representative—5 and 23. Table 15 indicates the relationships between type of organization and type of conflict in these districts. The conditions under which this type of board comes into being and the social milieu in which it operates do not lend themselves to the achievement of educational excellence.

The contributory factors for the white domination of a school board in a minority district rest squarely on the criteria for the creation of the districts—the registration, voting, age, and residency stipulations of the decentralization law.[23] The concept of heterogeneity in the law, though it held the promotion of school integration as its manifest aim, latently facilitated the gerrymandering of the districts' lines, so that it became impossible for blacks and Puerto Ricans to develop voting majorities. Secondly, the law's stipulation of open-voting

TABLE 15

Status Quo High-Conflict Boards

CSB	Composition			Pupil School Population				Voter Turnout		Type of Conflict
	PR	B	W	PR	B	W	O	Percent	Rank	
Unrepresentative School Boards										
1	3	1	3	71	15	9	5	15.0	12	CSB-Community
6	1	1	7	38	37	25	-	12.9	19	CSB-Community
9	3	4	2	40	45	15	-	7.4	28	B-PR
14	1	1	7	63	27	10	-	17.3	7	CSB-Community
28	-	3	6	6	41	53	-	12.2	20	CSB-Community
29	-	1	8	3	70	27	-			
Representative School Boards										
5	2	7	-	16	82	1	1	5.6	30	CSB-Community
23	1	8	-	28	71	1	-	4.9	31	CSB-Community

eligibility coupled with its age restriction further undermined the fundamental tenet of proportional representation, which essayed that voting was a prerequisite to representation.*

High-conflict districts are characterized by the presence of very many well-organized groups who view the school board as an imposition. The leaders of these groups are usually associated with or are employees of the poverty corporations in the community. In other cases, these leaders were the main actors during the life of the experimental districts. They graduated as professional activists during the teachers' strike of 1968 and, for the most part, were in the vanguard of change. These leaders who received their internship during the most difficult period of educational crisis in the city are not about to retreat from an unresponsive educational bureaucracy now peopled by different persons with the same attitude.

_____

*For a more detailed discussion of the impact of the law on the boards' composition, see Boulton H. Demas, The School Elections (New York: Institute for Community Studies, 1971), pp. 8-12.

Boycott of the elections is another characteristic reflected in the membership of some of these boards (for example, CSB's 23 and 29). Local leaders were wary of the weak decentralization law and argued that to vote in the school elections under such a law would be tantamount to aiding and abetting the bureaucracy in further depriving their children of quality education. As evidence of this, the low voter turnout (4.9 percent) in CSB 23 compares unfavorably with the 25 percent of eligible voters who participated in the elections for the old demonstration district governing board.

Furthermore, there seems to be a relationship of low voter turnout to the type of conflict. With only one exception, in all five minority districts where whites are overrepresented on the school board, the characteristic type of conflict is between the school board and the community. The one exception is CSB 9, where the conflict is between two oppressed minorities—blacks and Puerto Ricans. It is significant that this exception compares favorably to CSB's 5 and 23.

One remarkable difference, however, is that the CSB-community rift goes even further. It is between a black school board and a black community.

CSB 1

This district, which covers the Lower East Side in Manhattan, is an example of low voter turnout and a high degree of conflict. It is a community in which the ethnic public school population (71 percent Puerto Rican, 15 percent black, 9 percent white, and 5 percent Oriental) bears relationship to the distribution of population in the larger community. There are many more whites living in the community than the low 9 percent of the school population would seem to indicate. Because of the voting strength of whites who do not have children in the schools, the board initially was composed of six whites and three Puerto Ricans. The seething hostility of the Puerto Rican community might have subsided had the school board been insightful enough to build educational programs reflective of the aspirations of its school community. It did not, and that has led to the high degree of conflict between a white-dominated school board and the Puerto Rican community.

The conflict began when one of the white members, a priest, resigned. Many whites were visibly upset when the CSB appointed a black to fill the vacancy. The long-term split heightened their anxiety, but controversy erupted when another white member resigned, making minority control a more feasible goal. The board now had four whites, three Puerto Ricans, and one black. At this point, with a four to four split, the CSB became stalemated. The filling of this

vacancy became the cause célèbre in the district because both sides
wanted it to be filled by someone on their side.

While each segment of the CSB jockeyed for position, the controversy grew, like a ripple on a lake, encircling more participants.
Public meetings became boisterous scenes with shouting matches,
gavel-pounding, and contingents of policemen. As the stalemate
continued, the relationship between the Puerto Rican and white communities deteriorated. The Young Lords and the Jewish Defense
League confronted each other during the meetings and, after the
meetings, faced each other with chains, clubs, and brass knuckles.

It was alleged that the Puerto Ricans had adopted a strategy of
harassment to force the whites on the CSB to resign. To this end,
continued the allegation, the Young Lords sprayed the funeral parlor
owned by a white member with red paint. After the incident, she
resigned. To prevent the Puerto Rican community from profiting
from this advantage, the whites increased their militancy. They
solicited and received 325 applications for the two existing vacancies.
With a four-to-three split, now in favor of the Puerto Ricans, no item
could be decided upon.

At this point, in December 1971, Chancellor Scribner intervened
and mandated that the vacancies be filled by January 1, 1972. In the
event that his request was not met, two trustees would be appointed
as board members, and, with this makeshift complement, the CSB
would select two permanent members.

Again, both groups were at it. The whites wanted a general
election; the Puerto Ricans wanted appointments through the PA's
and the Presidents' Council. After some weeks of haggling, the
blacks gave in, and the trustee board appointed the two members:
one black and one white. The white community maintained that the
Chancellor's role was unconstitutional. The case is now before the
courts. And so the stalemate continues.

CSB 5

CSB 5 services the Central Harlem section of Manhattan. The
communities include Lower Park West, Upper Park West, Central
Harlem South, and parts of the Morningside-Manhattanville area.
Due to a partially successful boycott, only 5.6 percent of the eligible
registrants took part in the school board elections in 1969. They
elected a school board composed of seven blacks and two Puerto
Ricans.

The school board does not involve the community in the making
of educational policy at any level. Parents complain that both the
community superintendent and the school board are negligent in
informing the community with respect to general policies or to the

CSB's program of intent to raise the educational level of the students of the district.

As indicated elsewhere, CSB 5 includes the schools of the now defunct IS 201 experimental district. Included also are those leaders who had spearheaded the fight against the bureaucracy prior to and during the difficult days of the 1968 teachers' strike. Because of these leaders' contempt for the weak decentralization law, they boycotted the 1969 elections. Consequently, they became hostile to those who ran and won. The present members of the CSB would never have been there had the boycott group chosen to participate. The animus between the community school board and the community permeates and slows down the decision-making process of the CSB.

Because the community is supercritical of the CSB, the latter hardens its stance when dealing with the community. Recalcitrance on both sides results in disagreement on most issues. The result is that most public meetings at which executive CSB decisions are to be voted on usually become a melee that ends abruptly and chaotically. In only one decision did both the CSB and the community agree: the rejection of the community superintendent's 1972-73 budget. A further result of this breakdown is that the CSB had had only five open public meetings in the first eight months of 1972. Executive meetings are held once a week and are closed to the public.

The CSB chose a new superintendent upon assuming office. He has tried to dominate the school board, but often without success. Consequently his attempts have boomeranged and heightened the uneasiness between himself, the CSB, and the community. At the public meeting of December 16, 1971, for example, the CSB ordered rejection of his 1972-73 district budget on the grounds that he had failed to follow the procedures laid down by the budget committee of the school board and by the central Board. Procedures for the submission of annual budgets to the chancellor ask that both the chairman of the school board and the community superintendent append their signature and that the date of the public hearing be recorded. Board of Education records reveal no data on a public hearing, presumably because none was held. In addition, the only signator to the document was the community superintendent. Residents and parents of the community also complain about the tight lid that he has put on information.

In the area of budget, nothing has been done except the hiring of a business manager. An in-service program for paraprofessionals was instituted but has since been disbanded.

As to basic curriculum, no changes were attempted. The $5 million allocation of Title 1 funds was spent mostly on the centrally mandated programs, which obtained prior to decentralization, such as MES and SEC.

A few principals were hired, but the great majority came from names on the Board of Education lists.

CSB 6

     CSB 6 services the Upper West Side of Manhattan; it is grossly underrepresentative, for, with only a 25 percent white school population, there have been as many as seven white members of the CSB. Thus, a volatile situation hangs like a pall over community participation.

     In its first year of existence, the board managed to keep an uneasy peace with parents. It hired a new community superintendent and created some new programs under Title I, but it has involved parents more as a result of the aggressiveness of some PA's and militant community residents than out of a commitment to that procedure.

     Regarding principal selection, the initial interviews are conducted by the Parents' Association of the individual school. Upon completion of its interviews, the PA sends the names of its first three choices to the CSB; from that list the school board selects the applicant it thinks best qualified. According to a board spokesman, the following five steps were followed by the school board in the choosing of its community superintendent.

     1. The CSB advertised for the job in The New York Times and educational journals. Almost 100 applications were received.

     2. A parent-community screening panel to rate each applicant was selected. This panel was made up of one representative from each of 3 planning areas in the district. This made a panel of 6 community representatives and 13 parents.

     3. Of the applicants, 14 were rated excellent by this panel.

     4. Together with the community school board, the panel next narrowed the group down to three individuals.

     5. The community school board then selected one of these individuals to be the community superintendent.

     Dr. Edwin J. Haas, the community superintendent, was chosen after much talk on both sides, and many residents still feel that he was foisted upon them. He is criticized openly for lack of leadership and an inability to come up with concrete educational programs. The Presidents' Council and the Parents' Advisory Council have criticized him for the infinitesmally small contribution he makes to their meetings. At public meetings, he sits at the far end of the board's table. Even during the most heated controversies his opinion is neither solicited nor given.

     CSB-community hostility flared on a simple matter involving the sending of children to a summer camp in Vermont. The options were to send 60 children for 5 weeks or 75 children for 4 weeks. Some community representatives favored the latter option. The board overrode the desires of the community interests, sent 60 children for 5 weeks, arguing that it was not its intention to transfer the ghetto to Vermont.

Such unresponsiveness on behalf of the CSB to certain community interests has created a climate in which the ratification of the
minutes for the previous meeting takes an hour. Parents bring
verbatim reports of the last meeting to guarantee that nothing is
excluded. Nor is it uncommon for these groups to force the board to
take action. In one instance, the community wished to secure leases of
existing facilities in the district for vest-pocket schools. When the
central Board refused to act and the CSB was reluctant to protest,
parents led an organized boycott on the schools. Subsequently, the
CSB supported the boycott and the Board of Education made some
movement toward leasing the structures.

Conflicts in this district are primarily due to a school board
that is less change oriented than are certain active organized groups
in the community. Such groups are determined to make fundamental
changes, and, to this end, they formed a rump board. The crisis that
led to the formation of the rump board began at the November 1971
public meeting. The PA of PS 128 interviewed candidates for the
position of principal and selected two to serve in a joint capacity.
Legal questions over pay and designation were arranged. However,
the board refused to go along with the joint appointment, and a crisis
followed. Infuriated, the PA prevented the CSB from conducting any
other business until this question was decided. The CSB refused to
consider the case of PS 128 unless the meeting continued and declared
that it would only discuss the issue when it came up on the agenda.
With both sides unwilling to compromise, the deadlock persisted until
midnight, when police arrived to escort CSB members out of the
building.

Cooler heads never prevailed, both sides remained adamant, and
so the situation was never adequately resolved with the community.
This was only the beginning: The protests of the parents and alleged
threats to CSB members resulted in several public meetings' being
canceled because there was no quorum.

Another event that incensed the community and led to greater
CSB-community split was the attempt to fill a CSB vacancy that had
existed since late in the 1970-71 school year. As the 1971 summer
approached, progress slowed, as CSB 6 did not secure quorums.
Procedural arrangements for selection of the new member were not
finalized until the fall. Parents in the district were to be involved in
the appointment process. As in the selection of principals, however,
final decisions rested with the board.

The CSB asked for the advice of all the Parents' Associations
in the area. The parents and the community gave overwhelming
support to the candidacy of Ricardo Buchanan. Twelve of the 14 PA's
in the area endorsed his candidacy. The Presidents' Council in
District 6 also endorsed him. At the February 1972 public meeting,

which had on its agenda the appointment of the new member to the
CSB, the board did not have a quorum for the meeting. The community,
believing this to be an attempt to keep Buchanan off the board, became
enraged over yet another canceled meeting. It was at this point that
the community formed its own board: the People's Community School
Board.

Despite the formation of this rump board, its leaders appeared
at the regularly scheduled meeting of the other CSB in March 1972.
All eight members of the CSB were present. At this meeting, despite
the opinion of the community, the Parents' Associations, the president
of the Presidents' Council, and members of the rump board, the CSB
saw fit not to nominate Ricardo Buchanan. The chances of reconcilia-
tion between the CSB and the community were doomed.

Yet another example of the board's rigidity was its support of
programs to which the community was opposed. One such program
was "Open Door," a program designed to modify the violent and anti-
social behavior that some children had displayed in the classroom.
Some members of the community felt for the safety of their children
because the criteria for isolating disruptive children was too arbitrary.
Some even argued that the real intention of the CSB was political and
that the children of active parents would be the first to be called
disruptive. Despite public proclamations for rescinding the program
at the April, May, June, and September 1971 public meetings, the
CSB voted for the continued inclusion of the program in the budget.

Unlike other boards, this CSB has made no attempt to hire
personnel who do not appear on the ranked lists; nor has it tried to
establish new priorities for the district. Thus, the relationship
between the CSB and the community remains strained; important
educational policy decisions are not acted upon, and the low achievement levels of the pupils remain.

CSB 9

CSB 9 encompasses the Concourse and Morrisania communities
of the Bronx. The rather representative school board has four blacks,
three Puerto Ricans, and two whites; the student population is 45
percent black, 40 percent Puerto Rican, and 15 percent white.

Conflict between blacks and Puerto Ricans undermines the
effectiveness of the district. Some teachers have been working in the
district for little more than three years without receiving tenure
because of the continued disruption at public meetings. In 1971, two
monthly public meetings were postponed, and in April 1972 the date
of the monthly meeting was moved up twice.

The district has one innovative program—the Tarkington
Program. Though hailed by the community superintendent, UFT

President Albert Shanker reported that the program had a short life. An OEO administrator is quoted as saying that "the testing conditions for the performance contracting [the nucleus of the program] are intolerable and [result] in incomplete and invalid test scores." Whether the attacks on the program's efficiency are true or not, one fact has been documented: A large percentage of the machines are inoperative. An instructional program that places a great emphasis on machines could hardly be effective in such circumstances.

CSB 14

Here, the white population of Greenpoint voted into office a school board composed of six whites, one Cuban, one Puerto Rican, and one black. Of eligible voters, 17.3 percent participated in the school elections. The ethnic pupil distribution is 63 percent Puerto Rican, 27 percent black, and 10 percent white. Thus, in a situation where 90 percent of the pupils is represented by 33 percent of the school board, conflict is bound to develop.

Since the white members from Greenpoint feel that the schools in their area have functioned well over the years, issues dealing with busing and zoning are those that come up most often on the agenda. On these, the CSB's vote is always split 7-2 in favor of the members from Greenpoint.

The Puerto Rican community in the Williamsburg area is well organized. The leaders in the community are employees of the Williamsburg Community Corporation and other poverty agencies in the area. Disgusted by the board's recalcitrance in dealing with matters of concern to Puerto Ricans, they formed a rump board and occupied the seats on the podium reserved for the school board members.

When the "real" members arrived, they stood in the aisles and traded remarks with the rump board over the legality of the act. After about one hour, the "real" board members conferred among them themselves and announced their decision to go to another venue to hold the scheduled meeting. All but a handful of whites in the audience accompanied them to the new venue. Almost all the blacks remained to listen to the rump board and the Puerto Rican and black CSB member develop strategy for dealing with the new situation. In private, some members of the rump board claimed that they were surprised that the CSB had left. They thought that they would have remained to confront and debate the issues that the rump board had brought up.

The action of the Puerto Rican community may have been ill-timed, because, at the hastily found venue, the board adopted a resolution to hire as acting community superintendent a little-known person of Irish descent. Though the Puerto Ricans have since contested

the constitutionality of the board's action on that night, it seems likely
that the acting superintendent will be chosen as the permanent community superintendent.

One would think that after scoring this victory the CSB would
have exercised some measure of accountability when the issue of
filling a vacancy for principal in one of the Williamsburg schools
arose. But, to punish the Puerto Rican community, the CSB overrode
even the wishes of the white Greenpoint parents. Parents in both the
Greenpoint and Williamsburg communities had met and decided to
resist the CSB's decision to transfer the principal of a white school
in Greenpoint to the principalship of the black Williamsburg school
and upgrade the Greenpoint assistant principal to acting principal.

Although these conflicts took place after the community superintendent, Ralph Brande, had resigned, they were smouldering while
he was in office. He is considered to be quite capable and intelligent,
but he had confided to friends that he was tired of turmoil and brokerage
and was seeking less troubled waters. He is now the community
superintendent in CSB 22. There was only one dissenting CSB member
to his appointment in District 22.

CSB 23

This school board in Brownsville actively seeks to curtail community involvement. Policy is made by a few trusted partisans of the
chairman of the board. The school board is run like Tammany Hall,
rewarding its friends and punishing its enemies. Its friends are
among the 4.9 percent of the eligible voters who participated in the
school's elections. Considering that the chairman won by 75 proportional representation votes, the league of friends may constitute just
these few.

On the other hand, the board's enemies appear to be many.
Because the CSB does not tailor a broad policy to fit the education
needs of the community, the latter strikes back by constantly challenging the board.

In October 1971, an important brief was filed on behalf of 47
parents and organizations accusing the chairman and the school board
of misconduct. The report contained 133 pages and 182 exhibits
including affidavits. It asked the Chancellor to remove the board
"and appoint an interim three-man trusteeship appointed by him"
in consultation with the petitioners.[24]

The Chancellor appointed a Wall Street lawyer, Mahlon Perkins,
in October 1971 to submit recommendations with respect to the
charges and countercharges filed at that time by both sides. The
hearing officer allowed both sides more time to submit further
written reports to substantiate their charges.

Many of the new charges were similar to those made earlier,
but several had not come out before. The brief alleges that the board
paid over $500,000 to two security companies that are contributors
to the United Political Club (UPC), which is headed by the CSB chairman, without public disclosure of the inherent conflict of interest.
Further, these contracts were let although the companies were never
licensed to perform the services for which they had been contracted
and, in furtherance of this illegal act, the companies falsified vouchers,
violated state and board regulations, and exploited the CSB security
guards in order to maximize profits. It was also alleged that 160
employees of the district are members of or contributors to UPC.
These include the district's highest administrators, teachers, custodians,
and community people.

The New York Amsterdam News carried a detailed rundown of
the other charges, and it would be instructive to quote this article in
part.

> The District 23 school board has also rented real estate
> at exorbitant costs from principle officers in the UPC.
> One example cited is a building at 400 Stone Ave. . . .
> whose offices include Jules Zweibel, president of the
> UPC; Dominic Basso, vice president; and Jack Stegman,
> a contributor to UPC. Twelve days after the group pur-
> chased the building, the school board voted to rent the
> site as the district office.
>
> Another example of this type of transaction is . . .
> 1172 Pitkin Ave., described as "a dilapidated frame
> structure without running water, heat, toilet facilities
> and with floor caving in." This was rented by the dis-
> trict from the ACCT Holding Company for $10,800 a
> year.
>
> Basso is president of the company, Zweibel is vice
> president and Stegman and Koblin are officers. . . . In
> another instance, board member and UPC executive
> secretary Elmer Hamilton seconded a motion to hire an
> evaluation firm, Human Affairs Research Center [HARC],
> which was awarded contracts totalling several hundred
> thousand dollars to evaluate the district's state and
> federally-funded programs.
>
> Petitioners charge that Hamilton and HARC violated
> the Board of Education's Manual for Reimbursable Pro-
> grams, which prohibits a school board member from being
> "employed as a consultant when there is a conflict with his
> other employment or activities."

"All of the above actions involving the school board,"
says the report, "were taken by the board without disclosure of the conflict of interest and without a vote at a public meeting."
. . . Finally the report charges that Wright used school
board money "to directly benefit himself in his capacity as
an assemblyman and attorney," and that he placed many
UPC members in jobs in the district's $600,000 drug abuse
program.
In at least two instances, the report charges, school
board members received money as a result of their actions
on the board. Louis Brown, a board member and owner of
the Mattie Lou Real Estate Corporation, signed a receipt
for the board acknowledging delivery of fuel oil sold by
his firm. This fact alone, say the petitioners, "is sufficient
to order the removal of Brown as a member of the board."[25]

CSB 19

CSB 19 represents East New York and parts of Bushwick-
Ridgewood, Canarsie, Brownsville, and Bedford-Stuyvesant. It is a
fairly stable area, although East New York, Bushwick-Ridgewood,
and Canarsie are still growing and changing. With a combined student
minority population of 83 percent (50 percent black and 33 percent
Puerto Rican), the CSB is unrepresentative of the district. In the
1969 school board elections, 13.3 percent of eligible voters elected a
board composed of seven whites, one black, and one Puerto Rican.
All nine were college-trained and professionally oriented. As of
June 30, 1972, the two minority members had resigned. These
resignations occurred when the black and Puerto Rican community
was beginning to have an effective voice on the local council of
education.
Expectedly, the relationship between the white-dominated school
board and the mostly minority community over which its presides is
one characterized by suspicion and occasional outbursts of hostility.
The United Teacher of April 11, 1971 reported that the then community
superintendent, Elizabeth O'Daly, was physically abused and mentally
harassed during a demonstration in front of the district office on
March 31, 1971.[26] This animus between the school board and the
community results in escalating rigidity on both sides. On the one
hand, the CSB refuses to encourage the community's participation in
educational decision-making, and, on the other, the community angrily
protests this treatment at public meetings.
Community participation, as already indicated, is limited. The
CSB created procedures for the selection of acting supervisors. Its

memorandum is instructive in that it delineates in black and white
the board's feeble attempts to share decision-making with the community. When line vacancies for acting principals occur, the CSB
notifies the Office of Personnel at the Board of Education. All district
schools and the CSA are also notified. The memorandum says, in
part, that, at the time these and other notices are sent,

> a letter is sent by the Secretary of the Community School
> Board to the PTA President requesting parents' criteria
> for a principal. Under separate mailing, a letter is sent
> by the secretary to the PTA informing them of the pro-
> cedures involving the selection of a principal and advising
> them that three members of the PTA may sit in on inter-
> views in an advisory capacity only. Upon the conclusion
> of the interviews, parents are requested to submit 3 names
> in order of first, second and third choices. The Community
> School Board considers the choices and then, may or may
> not select an applicant consonant with the order of choice.
> They may, if they wish, select someone whom the parents
> have not nominated.[27]

The school board scrupulously adheres to its guidelines. There
were only two instances out of ten where the applicant chosen was
"consonant with the order of choice" of the community. The memorandum also carried three factors of applicant eligibility. They were
all geared to the traditionally accepted credentialed system:

> Candidates must have been eligible for the last principals'
> exam given by the Board of Examiners or
> Candidates must possess State Certification as a
> School Administrator with at least one year's administra-
> tive experience.
> Candidates must have had at least 5 years of class-
> room teaching experience.[28]

In another section of the memorandum, the CSB mandated that
the "transfer plan established by the CSA and Central Board of
Education will be followed in selection of both the acting principal
and other supervisory positions."[29]

Although the tenor of the board's memorandum speaks of performance objectives and evaluation criteria, its good intentions are
on the whole limited by its institutionalizing of the community as a
pariah in personnel selection.

Another index of the CSB's disregard of the community is visible
in the area of communication. Notices of public meetings are mailed

one week before the scheduled date of the meeting. Public meetings
are held once every month on the third Monday. At the start of the
1972-73 school year, the CSB expected to hold these meetings on third
Tuesdays. No reason has been advanced for the proposed change,
but one resident is assured that "it won't make any heck of a difference."
These public meetings begin with the pledge of allegiance to the flag.
The proceedings are taped. Written reproductions are not usually
made nor are tape recordings accessible for public listening. The
CSB made summaries of the January and February 1972 meetings and
circulated them. Copies are now unavailable, and those who have
them guard them jealously.

The CSB provides no alternative mechanisms for informing its
constituents. Open executive meetings are taboo. Closed executive
meetings are held once each week. As to public meetings, then, it
can be conclusively said that their main function is to apprise the
community of decisions made in private. The result of this practice
is the creation of charges and countercharges of what did or did not
occur at the last public meeting. Because the participants do not
have copies of the minutes to consult, debates on what happened at the
last meeting occupy the energies of both CSB and community residents.
At the February 28, 1972 meeting, one CSB member complained that he
was unaware that an item on the agenda was tabled at a prior meeting.
Under the open discussion item, this same CSB member lambasted the
board for not involving parents and for not conducting public meetings
more intelligently. One parent suggested that "we should remain at
home because public school board meetings are a mere sham. The
school board may as well write us a letter as to the disposition of
meetings."30

Upon assuming office the CSB reappointed the incumbent as its
community superintendent. At meetings her reports are short and
devoid of substance. At one meeting we attended, she had no report.
At another, she reported that three busloads of teachers, parents,
and other community residents had gone to the Board of Estimate as
a means of indicating community concern.

In the area of curriculum, the board has not deviated from
past procedures nor has it initiated any projects that would not have
been established under the centralized system. The new programs
include a black history course, a drug project, a physical education
course, and an after-school music course. These programs are
mandated for all city schools.

The area of personnel has also seen no drastic or even moderate
attempts to change established centralized procedures. The hiring
and firing of teachers still takes place under the centralized guidelines.

To keep abreast of monetary problems and effectuate a better
use of funds, CSB 19 has hired a full-time business manager. Except

here, the CSB stays well within the guidelines established by the
Board of Education.

CSB 28

CSB 28 includes Jamaica, South Jamaica, Briarwood, Ozone
Park, Richmond Hill, Kew Gardens, Springfield Gardens, Rochdale
Village, Forest Hills , and Rego Park. The pupil population is 6
percent Puerto Rican, 41 percent black; and 53 percent white. The
school board is composed of six whites and three blacks. The
percentage of eligible voters who elected the school board was median
compared to the city turnout: 12.2 percent.

CSB 28 is one of those districts where, although the larger
population is almost evenly divided between minority and whites, the
bulk of the public school children are blacks and Puerto Ricans.
Because of this, and exacerbated by the drawing of the district lines,
the school board is unrepresentative of the black population in the
district.

Parental involvement in the determination of budget, curriculum,
and personnel is virtually nonexistent. "The board acts in a way as
if it is invulnerable to attack. Its answers are always vague and
noncommittal. Even the Title I Advisory Committee has not been
consulted as it should." These were the remarks of one board member
in an interview of October 6, 1971.

Church influence is minimal. There was only one member who
ran on a parochial slate. It was reported that during a meeting held
to discuss budget cuts on December 30, 1971 both the UFT and CSA
district representatives were seated at the CSB table. It is rumored
that both unions will have representatives on the interviewing panel
to choose the next community superintendent. No attempt was made
by the CSB to hire teaching or supervisory personnel who are not on
the eligibility lists. The CSB defers to the community superintendent
and the professionals in the area of curriculum.

Black-white tension in the district is very high. The Shimer
Junior High School issue dominated the district throughout the first
year of decentralization. The charges and countercharges between
the CSB and a black female assistant principal spilled over into the
larger community and further polarized the district into hostile
ethnic camps. As a result, on the issues of busing, zoning, and CSB-
UFT contractural relationships, the vote on the CSB has been consistently split six to three in favor of the white CSB members.

Black participation is limited because of the CSB's policy to
hold all public meetings at JHS 217, which is in the white section of
the district and is not located near public transportation.

There have been no moves to change the basic curriculum, and
the allocations for Title I are spent mainly on the MES and SEC

programs. Tenure is routinely granted without parental input, but the
CSB refused tenure to five teachers whom many parents considered
to be competent.

Thus, the lack of representative community involvement has
created a black-white tension that pervades all board actions.

CSB 29

Community School Board 29 services Queens Village, parts of
Springfield Gardens, Hollis, Laurelton, Rosedale, and Jamaica. Though
its predominantly black population gave little support to the school
board elections, District 29 ranked eighth in voter turnout in the city.
Of its eligible voters, 16.6 percent participated in the elections and
voted in a school board of eight whites and one black. This pattern of
composition of the board is totally unrepresentative in view of the
ethnic distribution of the schools' population: 3 percent Puerto Rican,
70 percent black, and 27 percent white.

Though some members of the school board openly boast about
the high degree to which they involve the community in decision-making,
community involvement is almost nonexistent. The one isolated
example to which the CSB can point is the establishment of mini-
schools at PS 34 and PS 147 where site selection was made possible
through the efforts of two CSB members, who made telephone calls
to those with whom the board had wished to consult.

Conflict is clearly evident between the predominantly black
community and the almost white community school board. At open
public meetings black groups, together with feeble support from a
few white supporters, are most vocal in demanding accountability
from the board.

The black community complains of the board's unresponsiveness.
Complaints include virtual lack of inspection of the district's schools
by the CSB, inaccessibility of board members, poorly conceived and
poorly run Title 1 programs, and lack of community involvement due
to "across-the-board prejudice by the white members of the board
against black people." A black PTA president believed the board
perceived her as a nonentity and of inferior mental development.
She further contended that the board never listened either to her or
the PTA organization.

Because six members of the present board ran with the strong
backing of either Catholic or Jewish groups and because of the com-
placency of the black populace during the school elections, resolution
of black demands by the white-dominated school board seems a long
way off. The board remains stolid, hostile, and cynical toward the
black community.

During an interview, a CSB member ventured the hypothesis
that the most vocal of the black groups were funded by the federal

government under an umbrella program called the "Social Concern Committee" and that their sole function is to cause disruption. It was his feeling that acceptance of black demands is disadvantageous to the rest of the larger, and silent, community, which is in the majority.

In this impasse between the CSB and the community, the community superintendent sides with the school board. His relationship with the board is amicable. Only one board member voiced dissatisfaction with him. This member favors a replacement who is an "educator with detailed specialized knowledge."

The community superintendent works cooperatively with the board. This cooperation does not redound to the educational advantage of the children for, being white and a product of the system he now administers, he reinforces the school board's policies. One PTA member complained of the inability to get a straight answer out of him.

This unwitting conspiracy between the community superintendent and the board is not conducive to increased educational output. Curriculum has seen no significant input. The general attitude of the CSB in this policy area is summarized in a board member's reply to a question: "Curriculum," he said, "should be left to the professional educators." A second board member emphasized that "What the parents don't realize is that it is normal for half the children to score below grade level on reading, so in our district there is no great problem."

The CSB has hired a business manager, and the local board has blamed the central Board for budget cuts, while making no effort to reallocate any of its own resources.

In personnel, though parents sit in on interviews, they cannot directly question candidates for appointment. Seven principals who resigned have been replaced by applicants who were on the eligibility lists.

Convinced in its desire not to involve the community and dedicated to run a school system on traditional concepts, CSB 29 would be proud to be characterized as a status quo board.

Status Quo Boards
in White Districts

In these districts (11, 18, 20, 21, 22, 24, 25, 26, 27, 30, and 31) there is homogeneity with respect to pupil population and the composition of the school board. Other characteristics of white status quo boards are very little curriculum change, lack of community participation in the making of educational policy, high voter turnout during the school elections, and no hiring of personnel whose names do not appear on the eligibility list. (See Table 16.) Most significantly, due to the persistently high performance of the children in these districts, plus the numerous alternatives open to those children who perform poorly, the members of these school boards have very little desire or motivation to buck the system; after all, it was this same system that helped them achieve their social mobility.

Of the 13 white traditional school boards, 7 are all white and 2 (10 and 11) have 1 Puerto Rican and 1 black member respectively. CSB 22 is unusual. Covering the Midwood and Sheepshead Bay sections of Brooklyn where there are few minority people (11 percent pupil population), CSB 22 has appointed one black male to its board. Rumor has it that this was due to an effort to imbue the board with a posture of progressivism, but the board may well have since regretted this action because this seemingly safe black has caused some modicum of intraboard conflict. Though he may merely be playing the devil's advocate, he has raised many real and substantive issues. In spite of this, CSB 22 rides roughshod over his demurrers.

There is very little open conflict between the school board and the community. This is due to the consistently high performance of the children on the Metropolitan Achievement Tests. Coupled with this factor is the virtual absence of low-income blacks and Puerto Ricans and their traveling companion—the syndrome of poverty, disease, underachievement, Title I funds, and poverty agencies.

There is very little community involvement. The PTA's are, for the most part, active only in crisis situations. They lack the extra official involvement that Title I gives to some poorer communities. Thus, they conform to the traditional mold of sponsoring cake sales and providing coffee for the principals. The acceptance and interpretation of their role as a traditional one even under the new decentralization law contributed to the situation where most of the time the board takes them for granted. In one case, however, a PTA was piqued at the board's failure to consult it in the hiring of a principal. It flexed its muscle, brought suit against the school board, but lost the case on a legal technicality.

Teaching personnel are consistently taken from the eligibility lists; no teacher or principal was ever refused tenure. This reflects a willingness to conform to the traditional guidelines of the Board of Education and a narrow interpretation of contractual obligations.

CSB 11

CSB 11, located in the northeastern corner of the Bronx, includes Pelham Bay, Williamsbridge, and Morris Park. The Catholic church is very influential. Though the district is no longer all white, black involvement in the school is minimal. At some meetings the number

TABLE 16

White Status Quo Boards

| CSB | Pupil Population | | | CSB Composition | | | Information Distribution | | | | No cir. results | Old Superintendent Rehired | 1971 Average MAT 5th-Grade Reading Scores | Off-List Hiring | |
| | | | | | | | Open Executive Meetings | | Newsletter | | | | | | |
	PR	B	W	PR	B	W	Yes	No	Yes	No				Yes	No
11	12	33	55	1		8		x		x	x	x	6.4		x
18	7	31	62			9		x		x	x	x	5.4		x
20	10	11	79			9		x		x	x	x	5.3		x
21a	8	11	81			9		x		x	x	x	5.3		x
22b	2	9	89	1		8		x		x	x	x	6.4		x
24	16	13	71			9		x		x	x	x	5.5		x
25	4	9	87			9		x		x	x	x	6.4		x
26	2	13	85			9		x		x	x	x	6.5		x
27b	4	28	67			9		x		x	x	x	5.1		x
30c	14	20	66			9		x		x	x	x	5.7		x
31d	3	8	87			9		x		x	x	x	6.4		x

aData for three schools missing.
bData for one school missing.
cData for four schools missing.
dData for six schools missing.

Sources: Interviews with CSB members and community residents; The New York Times, March 8, 1972; the United Parents' Association, 1970.

of blacks in the audience totals less than 10. With a minority pupil population of 45 percent (12 percent Puerto Rican and 33 percent black), it is easy to account for the continued traditional style in which the CSB conducts its business.

Typical of white middle-class school board meetings, there are prepared agenda of nonitems, well-taken minutes, etc. Public meetings are held regularly. Two meetings were held in one month. These meetings are used to advise the public on the merits of the educational system as it is. No dialogue is allowed. Geared to pre-empt community involvement or conflict, these lackluster, orderly meetings average only 45 minutes.

The CSB's relationship to both its community superintendent and the central Board is excellent. All see eye to eye on most issues.

With no Title I schools in the district, with only $80 per child following those who are bused in, and with the passivity of the minority community, compensatory programs are almost nonexistent. The only other extra funds come to the district in the form of a drug-prevention program.

The basic curriculum remains virtually untouched; hiring of personnel not on the eligibility lists is unthinkable.

CSB 18

CSB 18 services Canarsie and parts of the East Flatbush section of Brooklyn. In the school elections of 1969, 17.4 percent of the eligible voters elected an all-white school board. Thus, the composition of the school board does not reflect the ethnic distribution of the almost 14,000 elementary school pupils within this district, where 38 percent (Puerto Rican: 7 percent; black: 31 percent) of the pupil population is from minority groups.

Community involvement is infrequent and is limited to site selection. This was evidenced in the selection of the site for IS 387. In the area of personnel, the community is given a minimal consultative role. Instances where the parents' and board's choice coincide is due more to a fortuitous combination of circumstances than to a reflection of the board's effort to involve the community as a partner in decision-making.

Spokesmen for the school board perceive the legal requirement for community participation as a deterrent to the smooth (nonissue-oriented) functioning of the board. They ascribe their lack of innovation to "disruptive" tactics of certain elements in the community.

Furthermore, community residents have reported that the conduct of public meetings leaves much to be desired. Some members of the board enjoy little respect from the community, due probably to the board's attitude of aborting dialogue on controversial (zoning, busing) issues. A member of the audience was heard to say, at a public meeting, "if it wasn't for Mr. Garner [the community superintendent] who is genuinely concerned and personally guarantees action on all questions, one might find a community school board without a community."

The school board, upon assuming office, rehired the incumbent superintendent. Though the CSB was not committed to any radical departure from the old way of doing things, it was ahead of its superintendent. It therefore seized the opportunity, upon his resignation, to appoint a man whose orientations are less anachronistic.

The new community superintendent's relationship to the school board is reasonably good, but slightly strained. He tries, with limited success, to dominate the board so that he can push its members to the brink of educational progressivism. Their resistance creates some uneasiness between him and some members on the CSB. Despite these handicaps, the superintendent is considered the savior of the district by many people. Moreover, he has established and lent his weight to many new programs.

The tone of this district is a conservative one; changing traditional standards does not come easily to the members of this school board, and, as already indicated, attempts often engender intraboard conflict. Consequently, the major issues of the board are zoning and busing. For example, zoning of a high school was the main agenda item of the public meeting of March 1972. Over 700 persons were in attendance. This is an alarming turnout in view of the fact that the average attendance at these meetings in this district is usually under 300, with well over 60 percent being teachers and other pedagogical personnel employed by the district. To date, the zoning of this high school is still unresolved.

Because of the district's basic conservative strain coupled with the fact that the majority (white) of the pupils perform well on the Metropolitan Achievement Tests, innovation in basic curriculum has not taken place. The district expends most of its Title I funds on SEC and Head Start but also runs Project Success, Block School for Pre-Schoolers, a Mobile Industrial Art Program, and its Academic Cultural Vocational Program for youth (PS's 219, 232, 235, and 252).

In personnel and budget matters the district has been very traditional; a budget officer has not been hired. Five principals have been hired since decentralization, all were on the lists and all are white.

CSB 20

CSB district 20 consists of Bay Ridge, parts of Borough Park, and parts of Bensonhurst. Of the total 158,922 voters, only 30,575 went to the polls, representing a meager 19.2 percent. When compared to the predominantly black districts, however, it was an impressive turnout, ranking third in the entire city and tying with CSB 25, another predominantly white district.

Though the minority student population is 21 percent (10 percent Puerto Rican and 11 percent black), the school board is all white. The black-white-Puerto Rican relationship is not at present a problem because so few parents in the district are either black or Puerto Rican. As a matter of fact, the 21 percent black and Puerto Rican pupil population is concentrated in PS 140 and PS 164 and is representative of children bused in form "ghetto" areas or brought in on an open-enrollment basis. The one noteworthy incident occurred when the Title I advisory committee, whose membership is largely black, accused the CSB of using Title I monies to finance a district newspaper.

The CSB claims that it involves the community in educational decision-making. It points to the selection of narcotics coordinators and the ratification of the parents' choice for principal vacancies as examples of community participation.

Parental input on special committees can be documented, but such a program is so peripheral to the development of sound educational policy that parental involvement is negligible. To begin with, the program had a budget of $398,000. A special committee was created to appoint a director, secretary, and program coordinator. This committee was composed of three CSB members, in addition to the chairman, the district superintendent, any parent who was desirous of becoming a member, one representative each from the UFT and CSA, and members of the CSB's own narcotics committee. Specifically, the committee was to screen the 28 applicants and recommend its choice to the CSB, who would make the official appointment. As it turned out, the person recommended was appointed by the CSB with not one dissenting vote. As to the appointment of the 22 full-time narcotics coordinators, they were chosen by the same process. Here, there was an additional community input: The principal and the parents of each school to which a coordinator was assigned were listened to carefully as to the selection of its coordinator.

The chairman of the board proudly pointed out that a well-qualified applicant for a vacant bilingual post was not named to the post for some time because the community had not had the opportunity to screen him.[31]

The parents of this community are not involved in the decision-making process. There are an overwhelming number of Catholics living in this district. Add to this the overrepresentation of professionals on the CSB (three lawyers, one priest, one rabbi, one high school teacher), and the limited participation afforded public school parents becomes evident.

Public meetings are used to bring to the attention of the public proposals and resolutions on which the CSB has already acted. Five minutes are given to parents for questions and/or comments after each committee report. The chairman of the CSB invokes parliamentary procedures rigidly to prevent members of the audience from making exhortatory remarks to the CSB.

On most occasions the CSB does not listen to the community. The reason may be because opinions from the community are so contradictory that they cancel each other out, thus leaving the CSB in the position of going through with its already arrived-at decision. Also, though the PTA is a viable group, it is largely composed of white middle-class parents, who can provide alternative ways of coping with the educational establishment and who thus perceive some problems as not being serious. This attitude renders their input and their attack on the CSB feeble gestures.

In no other CSB district to our knowledge does there exist such a thorough communication network between the CSB and the community as in CSB 20. There are three local newspapers in this district, and each dedicates one full page to the CSB each week. One of these papers, the Home Reporter, is reputed to have the largest circulation for local press coverage in New York City. Added to this, there is another infrastructure of communication that takes place through local organizations and those that are connected with education. CSB 20 is mainly a white-collar district in which many of the residents have overlapping memberships in different organizations, so that each often disseminates educational information to comembers of other groups not directly connected with education. For example, during the budget crisis, the CSB wanted to bring pressure on the district's legislators not to vote for any increased cuts; the communication channels were opened: priests called for help from their pulpits; letters were sent home to parents by their children; PTA meetings were specially scheduled; and the newspapers were alerted. Within one week, 20,000 letters were sent to the legislators, resulting in only one legislator's voting for increased cuts.

Minutes of public meetings are well-prepared photo offsets. Notices of public meetings detailing agenda items are sent out to the public about ten days prior to the date of the meeting.

Open public meetings are held on the third Tuesday in every month in accordance with the district's by-laws. To date no month has passed without such a meeting. Again in accordance with the district's by-laws, executive meetings are held at least once a week. In one recent month, the CSB experimented with two open executive meetings. Though two CSB members claimed that those were two of the worst executive meetings, some parents thought that it was a good idea to focus on the process by which CSB members make decisions.

One CSB member confided after one of these meetings that another
member who was always obstreperous at the closed executive sessions
was less so at the open meetings.

Upon assuming office the CSB reappointed the incumbent district
superintendent as its community superintendent. The relationship
between the CSB and the community superintendent is good. She does
not seek to dominate the board nor does it seek to dominate her.

The CSB is composed of members with such diverse professional
training that there are two competing and prevailing perceptions of
the community superintendent's relationship to the CSB and the community. Those on the CSB, such as Joseph Seminara, Reverend
Michael French, Rabbi Zalman Diskind and Andrew Sichenze, think
that the community superintendent is somewhat reactionary. As a
consequence, they perceive her relationship to the board as one of
calm hostility and to the community as one of aloofness. At public
meetings she is usually silent unless addressed or unless she is
scheduled to make a report. At the executive meetings, however, she
unmasks herself. For instance, the CSB became worried about a
change made by the Title I education advisory council, which had
agreed that the CSB had illegally used Title I funds for putting out a
district newspaper. The Title I coordinator said that, from his knowledge, such an expenditure was illegal; a practicing attorney and board
member said he was unwilling to have the CSB involved in a test case
on this matter, but the community superintendent countered by saying
that if things became difficult the CSB can always "swing it." She further reminded the CSB that the function of the education advisory
council is "purely advisory" and should not be taken too seriously.

In curriculum there are no accomplishments beyond what the
old centralization would have done. The only action taken is the
publication of a 15-page booklet on the district's educational needs.
The curriculum committee, in presenting this booklet, stated that it
was the "responsibility of the Curriculum Committee to oversee what
is being taught and how it effects the children both collectively and
individually. It is a great task before us particularly since our society
is in a great state of change. It is our hope that with constructive
work our committee will be sensitive to these changes."

The district has hired only those on the eligibility lists. There
is no one undergoing in-service training in the district.

CSB 21

CSB 21 includes six members who were endorsed by the Roman
Catholic church during the school elections. The board immediately
rehired the incumbent superintendent. The influence of the church
on educational decision-making and on the board's basic status quo
orientation is observable in the operation of the district.

Parent participation in the selection of principals is limited
to queries directed to members of the board. Public discussion is
discouraged and is limited to comments on such peripheral issues as
procedure. The rationale of the board is that some parents use public
meetings as a forum for making long political speeches.

This tone of the board permeates even the board's action on the
type, frequency, and method of distributing information. One CSB
member commented that "The more sparse the information, the less
likelihood is there of creating division in the community."[32] There
are no mailings. The board claims it wants to save money. Minutes
of public meetings are not reproduced. Community residents desirous
of securing information must go to the board's office to do so.

With an old-line community superintendent, with established links
to the conservative leaders in the community, and with a school board
dominated by members who ran on a church slate, the position of the
professionals is sacrosanct. Both community superintendent and
community school board in explaining their reluctance to involve
parents in school matters concurred that "tenure must be granted
quickly to preserve morale."[33]

There has been no observable move away from the earlier
method of selecting personnel from ranked lists. The CSB frowns
upon the Mansfield decision, which invalidated existing lists. The
only change in budget procedures is the hiring of a business manager.
Curriculum has seen only changes that would have been made under
the old system; among these are remedial reading, learning through
games, and a special program for "disruptive" children.

CSB 24

CSB 24 covers Maspeth and Middle Village, communities with
a high Catholic population. Though few board members are Catholic,
the CSB reflects the basic conservative tone of the district. Parental
participation is minimal despite the board's organization into nine
committees. Each committee is headed by a school board member
with two UFT representatives, two CSA representatives, and as many
parents as are willing to join.

Parental apathy is suggested by the CSB as the reason for the
low rate of parent involvement. Some residents of the district explain
minimum participation by the dominance of the community superintendent in the affairs of the district—plus the lack of candor on behalf
of the majority of the school board members. For the example, the
appointment of a drug coordinator took place without parents' having
prior knowledge that a vacancy existed. It was only after some parents strongly opposed this move that the community superintendent
condescended to enlighten parents on the qualifications of the chosen

applicant. In the selection of principals, parents have little input because the personnel committee hardly ever meets.

In keeping with the climate in which the school board conducts its business, the community suffers from a dearth of information. Beyond meeting announcements, which never amount to more than two pages, and an occasional newsletter, the district distributes little information. The superintendent controls most of the district's business. He speaks more than any one else at public meetings. Though Board of Education guidelines call for two signatures on budget reports submitted, his signature is the only one that consistently appears. Community residents interviewed complained that he was the main contributing cause for the reluctance of the board to discuss hard issues or make innovation in policy areas.

There has been no change in personnel practice since the board took office. The only departure in this area involved the appointment of bilingual teachers. Beyond a family-living course and the bilingual program no other curriculum changes have taken place. The budget cuts were taken as a calamitous event, yet no effort was expended to deal with this matter.

CSB 25

The CSB rehired the incumbent as its community superintendent when it assumed office in 1969. It does not involve the community in the making of educational policy, and no change has been made in the selection of pedagogical personnel.

A board member noted, "the community should not be involved in the granting of tenure. This is a professional matter."[34] Nor are parents involved in other areas of policy. The board ignored large segments of the community when it banned Piri Thomas's book Down These Mean Streets and diverted public funds to Catholic schools. At the public meeting at which these issues were discussed, all but a few parents and community residents argued against the board's decision to ban the book. Notwithstanding the public pressure, the CSB passed the resolution against the book five to four. Outraged at the CSB's disregard, fifteen parents brought litigation to enjoin the board from pursuing the banning. The court held for the defendants, arguing that the general power to determine curriculum includes the power over the selection of reading matter and that the power over curriculum rests with the CSB according to the stipulation of the decentralization law.

The community was deeply torn and incensed at the board's orientation. When, however, the CSB again voted five to four to pass its resolution to give public funds to Catholic schools—and this despite the articulated opposition of the community—a permanent rift developed

between the CSB and a large group of parents. Even those members
of the board who constitute the permanent minority came in for verbal
abuse from members of the board's majority faction. "Certain left-
wing elements on this board . . . are less educated than the rest of
the board. There is much disagreement because these four members
direct their actions toward public relations rather than to go along."[35]
The minority faction on the board has pushed for a greater parental
role and educational innovation.

Parochial dominance of the school board seems to dictate many
of the decisions of the board, which conform more to the religious and
moral sensibilities of the majority faction than to the educational needs
of the pupils. This moralistic proclivity, with its conservative overtones, has created an amicable relationship between the CSB and the
UFT and CSA. The UFT district chairman and union representatives
are consulted on all issues, while parental involvement remains limited.
Teachers are granted tenure uniformly; no pedagogical personnel
whose name does not appear on the ranked list has ever been hired.
Budgetary or personnel innovations are nonexistent. As for curriculum,
a much-touted Elementary-Nature-Science-Ecology Course has been
developed. Except for this course, the basic curriculum remains
unchanged.

CSB 26

Nestled in the communities of Douglaston and Bayside, CSB 26
serves probably the most well-to-do residents of any school board in
the city. It rehired the old superintendent, to whom it defers regularly.
The parents' deference to professional educators is understandable
because most of the parents and residents who live in this district
are professionals of one kind or another. As a result there is little
parental involvement in the granting of tenure or in the hiring of
pedagogical personnel.

In the selection of principals, parents sit in on the board's interview of the applicants but are not permitted to question the candidates directly, though at times their opinions might be solicited.
The lack of community involvement creates no conflict in the district
because one is given to believe that the community's support of the
CSB is one of willful compliance.

Relations with the UFT and CSA are amiable, and both groups
are consulted in almost all decisions. Tenure is granted uniformly
to teachers, and all personnel comes from central lists. There is
little noticeable innovation in budget and curriculum. The district
did solicit funds under Title III for an alternative junior high school,
which incorporates some elements of the alternative mini-high schools
and would serve the "advantaged" children on the district.

CSB 27

CSB 27 includes the communities of Rockaway, Woodhaven, Richmond Hill, South Ozone Park, Ridgewood, Maspeth, and Middle Village. The board (eight whites and one black) is reasonably representative of the ethnic pupil population distribution (67 percent white, 28 percent black, and 5 percent Puerto Rican). Parents actively participate in the discussion of issues at public meetings and the board welcomes this participation. Notices and agenda of open public meetings are sent seven to ten days in advance.

The black and Puerto Rican residents are passive. The school board grants tenure to teachers routinely and does not hire personnel who are not on the eligibility lists. The board's conflict with the central Board has been over problems that are system-wide, such as school construction, budget deadlines, supplies, etc. Program input is dominated by professionals, and there is no program that deviates significantly from the traditional line.

CSB 30

CSB 30 covers the communities of Jackson Heights, Astoria, Woodside, Elmhurst, and Long Island City. The school board is unrepresentative of district school population. It is an all-white board in a district whose school population is 14 percent Puerto Rican, 20 percent black, and 66 percent white. A sizable portion of the white population is Greek, Rumanian, Yugoslav, Polish, etc. Of the eligible voters, 13.4 percent elected the board.

This is a traditional board. Community participation is erratic. Parents were not involved in the filling of a board vacancy. In no case has the CSB permitted parents to see the résumés of candidates applying for the position of principal until the night of the interview. Yet the CSB has always ratified the choice of the PA. This is because the PA and CSB share identical views, and not because of CSB's responsiveness to community involvement. Minutes of public meetings are not distributed but can be perused at the CSB's office Monday through Friday.

The CSB has amiable relations with both the UFT and CSA. Both unions had representatives on the screening panel for the community superintendent; they are also represented on screening panels for principals. Blacks and Puerto Ricans hardly ever attend meetings. Since the vacancy on the CSB was filled by another white, some public meetings have no blacks at all. Tenure is granted routinely to teachers. Principals are chosen from the eligibility lists. In general, the CSB frowns on the new policy of appointments under the Mansfield decision.

No change has taken place in the basic curriculum and none is contemplated. The allocation for Title I is $928,165 for the 1971-72 school year. Expenditure on new programs has not occurred because of the low participation of the blacks and Puerto Ricans and the basic conservativeness of the school board.

CSB 31

CSB 31 covers the entire borough of Richmond. The student population includes 3 percent Puerto Rican, 8 percent black, and 89 percent white. The school elections saw a very high turnout of voters, the second largest in the city, with 18.2 percent of eligible voters taking part.

This unusually heavy vote elected an all-white community school board comprising of two Catholic priests, three Catholic laymen, three Protestants, and one Jew.

This is a very traditional board. In terms of knowledge, contacts, responsibility, and experience, it sees itself as an elite. Because of this, the board makes educational policy independently of the community. It plays no favorites to any particular white groups, but the Catholic representation on the board and the lack of minority representation works to the advantage of the one and the disadvantage of the other.

Parents are allowed to sit in on the interviews for hiring principals, but they cannot ask questions or make suggestions. This board was one of the last to use the Board of Education manual "Parents Association and the Schools." It threatened to go to court to prevent its use. Minutes are not made available to the public. They are taken verbatim and no digests are made. However, they can be read at the CSB's office Monday through Friday.

CSB union membership is strong. Staten Island residents are, for the most part, civil service employees, teachers, policemen, and firemen. Their understanding and respect for the merit system is supportive of the establishment-oriented school board. Because of this CSB-community problems are settled privately, and any disaffection of the board is communicated as gossip.

Thus, the only groups that are alienated are the blacks and Puerto Ricans, who are concentrated on the North Shore. Their main complaint is the de facto segregation that keeps them from the better schools and housing on the southern part of the island.

Expectedly, basic curriculum is untouched; Title I programs still are dominated by professionals. The community superintendent handpicks the chairman for each Title I project, and, even under the new federal ruling, professional input has not changed radically.

Teacher tenure is granted uniformly; dismissals are rare; one principal was hired who was not on the lists; but, despite this, CSB 31 continues to trudge the paths of educational tradition.

CONCLUSION

The main distinguishing feature between change-agent and status quo boards is the degree to which conflict has arisen between the boards and parents over school policy. This criterion is especially significant in personnel selection, a problem area exacerbated by ambiguities in the decentralization law, the provisions of the Mansfield decision, and parental recognition of the power to hire key personnel such as principals. Indeed, the power to hire, select, or assign principals is a significant power resource, and both parents and boards recognize it as such. The Mansfield decision permits a radical departure from the old policy, whereby CSB's had to select supervisory personnel from the Board of Examiners' eligibility list. Some school boards, notably the change-agent ones (3 and 13), have fully exploited this opportunity. Respectively, they appointed 11 and 13 persons to such positions. Some active boards have also shown a willingness to appoint personnel who are not on the lists. The exercise of such imagination and the willingness to be responsive had served to tighten the bond of cooperation between change-agent boards and the community.

In contrast, other CSB's (mainly status quo boards in high-conflict districts) are unwilling to involve parents meaningfully in personnel selection for fear that parents would usurp this power, the jealous guardianship of which causes strained relationships to develop between the communities and the boards.

Another reason for the conflict between the school boards and the community stems from the faulty and inadequate electoral mechanism. The mandate of the decentralization law that "every registered voter residing in a community district and every parent of a child attending any school under the jurisdiction of the community board of such district who is a citizen of the state, a resident of the city of New York for at least ninety days and at least twenty-one years of age shall be eligible to vote at such election for the members of such community board" opened the way for the capture of the school boards by groups whose views are antithetical to the interests of public education. The law sought to offset this possibility by conducting a special registration drive for parents of public school children who did not meet the strict residency qualification of the law. When all factors are considered, however, the bill's stipulation of open-voting eligibility to all residents was counterproductive to providing an environment free from conflict in which parents and the CSB could work together in making educational policy for the district.

The registration drive produced only minimal results. In every borough there were more newly registered voters than parents. There

were 25,426 newly registered regular voters as compared to 15,035
specially registered parent voters. Had the Bundy plan been instituted,
many of the problems that today plague the school boards would have
been avoided. The Bundy plan called either for a direct election process limited to parents only or a mixed "elective-appointive" process.
The limitation of board membership to only parents of public school
children was not upheld. It was the concern of many that education
is too vital a community-wide interest to exclude residents who are
not parents from membership on these boards. Moreover, community
school boards "should not be deprived of the special skills, experience,
interests or insights of parents whose children have finished school
or do not yet have children in the schools or even other capable
residents who are not parents."[36] This dual election process, whereby
all groups would be represented without the dangers of direct election,
was also not adopted. The objections were that the Bundy procedures
were too complex and that the safeguards for effective parental
representation could be easily subverted by one of the six democratic-
ally elected members' siding with the appointed bloc of five members.

Direct elections was the method adopted by the Albany legislators
and incorporated into the decentralization bill. The proponents of this
mechanism reasoned that, since the local boards were to have direct
control of expenditures, any mechanism short of direct elections
would be tantamount to taxation without representation. This argument
of taxation without representation was refuted by many on the grounds
that the districts would not have taxing powers and that the voters
would still retain the right to express their sentiments on taxation
for schools when electing city and state officials.

The opponents of direct election warned of the danger of domination by political clubs, the expense to candidates of campaigning, the
distastefulness of election campaigns to men and women who would
otherwise be willing to serve on the community school boards, and
the possible domination of school affairs by majorities of residents
who were not parents or by sectarian interests that might not hold
the interests of public education uppermost.[37] Because the Bundy
plan's warning was not heeded, the effects of the legislature's decision now plague the community school boards.

6

In evaluating one of the few operational plans for decentralization in the country at this time, we have often felt an understandable pressure to respond to the overwhelming rhetoric on both sides of the controversy. Widespread discussion of decentralization without evidence to support conclusions is common practice and increases the need for evaluation results. The character and purpose of decentralization, however, suggests the need for more long-range, clearly defined evaluation.

Because decentralization has not been implemented, the few plans that can be reasonably labeled as efforts at decentralization become all the more important to the debate. The division of power between the central agency and the local board is the key determinant of the output of decentralization. The extent to which power has been delegated to the local board provides the setting for institutional change, if it is to occur. If the power is not specifically delegated, it can be assumed by the local agent.

This confrontation with a central institution to force a redistribution of power is viewed by many analysts of decentralization as one of its great negatives; for others it represents a part of a necessary process. This suggests the strong value element in any attempt to evaluate the effectiveness of any decentralization plan. Decentralization can be measured in a number of ways. What the researcher chooses to measure, however, reflects his own value system. It implies what he thinks should be the output. If efficiency is the goal (a product most political scientists have long considered important), the evaluator will look at service delivered as compared to cost. Did it improve under decentralization? If the goal is improved service, measures have to be developed to determine whether or not change in the delivery and character of the service has occurred under the new arrangement.

In a particular functional area such as education, student achievement may be viewed as the goal; test scores then would be the standard measures. Obviously, it is simpler to measure output if the researcher sets up a single measurable goal and, particularly, if he can use some well-defined instrument to show results. In most cases, however, the measurement of social policies are far too complex and cannot be narrowed to a single simple output. Further adding to the difficulty is the lack of sophisticated instruments to measure the more complex kinds of changes one might think particularly relevant.

New York City school decentralization was at best a minimal plan. It fits the definition of political decentralization, as contrasted to administrative decentralization, only because it provided for the election of local boards that were to exercise some narrow policy-making powers. The powers specifically delegated by the legislation were nominal; most important was the power to appoint the community superintendent and school principals. If a major court decision had not allowed local boards to by-pass the Board of Examiners' principals list, the local boards' powers in the selection of principals would have been limited only to those lists. The Mansfield decision, however, gave an added dimension to the power of local boards. They could recruit and appoint a principal without his undergoing the traditional screening and examination.

The aim of school decentralization in New York was to redistribute power in the school policy process, giving local boards and communities control over their schools. It sought to achieve a basic change in the method of making decisions, increasing the participation of parents and community residents. These changes were intended to improve the quality of education through new programs and improved attitudes. This evaluation has been organized to determine the extent to which these goals have been achieved. Clearly measuring these kinds of outputs is more difficult than simply looking at educational achievement. We consider a change in student achievement an important goal of school decentralization but recognize that it is more likely to be a long-range product of the other outputs we seek to measure. It should be made clear, however, that if student achievement is not improved over a reasonable period of time one must conclude that decentralization is a failure.

This two-year analysis of school decentralization scrutinizes a minimal plan; its output expectedly reflects the limited intent of those who devised the plan. There have been no major changes in the distribution of power in school decision-making. Educational policy in New York City still depends on school professionals in their unions and associations under central contracts and agreements. The central headquarters staff and the Board of Education retain the major share of power. As indicated in the analysis, therefore, little has happened in the districts and in the schools. Our district-by-district rundown is disheartening in this regard. Only two district boards have been labeled "change agent." Those boards have seen themselves as school policy-makers; they have engaged the public in decision-making and changed procedures for selecting professional staff. They have encouraged the development of new programs and view this as a means to achieving quality education. The larger number of local boards are, however, clearly status quo oriented, willing to accept the traditional role of school professionals and the central staff. They have made no effort to change the delivery of educational services. In some of those districts internal political conflict has stalemated all action.

Despite the poor showing of the majority of local boards, there are some general signs of change worthy of mention. Citizen participation in school affairs has increased, particularly in more lower-class neighborhoods. Attendance at board meetings has improved and parent interest has heightened. There is considerable interest with the 1973 election and the need to run candidates for the local school board.

Parent organizations in several districts became involved directly in the selection of principals. Close to 300 new principals, many without traditional credentials, will be running schools in the city in 1973. The accomplishments of this new breed of principal, to be measured over the next two to four years, should suggest the scope and value of these changes. Clearly, community-selected principals will be community-oriented, and their loyalty will be to the local agency rather than to the central headquarters.

Although new educational programs are not widespread, there has been increased discussion of educational options and new methods that might be tried, particularly in schools that are failing. In selected districts teachers have been screened, and accountability is viewed as a necessity; how to achieve it is a matter of some concern. The major impact of parents has been felt in programs with federal and state funding where city budget and contract constraints do not exist. The Title I procedures, as noted, have been radically changed, and in many districts community involvement has greatly increased.

Local boards are represented in the contract negotiations, but it is too early to determine what their role will be. One of the representatives of the local boards in these negotiations has indicated his desire that local board powers not be negotiated away in the contract.

The positive results of the two-year experience of decentralization do not warrant great optimism. What must be recognized is that the limitations of the law were overwhelming. The 1969 decentralization law failed to grant to community school boards sufficient powers to enable them to operate their schools. Instead, the statute created a system with authority to run the schools divided among the central

Board, the chancellor, and the community school board. The powers and jurisdiction granted to the community school boards were made subject to other provisions of the decentralization law, many of which grant very substantial control to the chancellor, subject to the policies established by the city Board and subject to centrally made collective bargaining agreements.

Although it is conceivable that such a division of authority could have been formulated and drafted in a clear and workable manner, in fact the statute did not do so. It is a basic and vital flaw of the decentralization law that the grant of jurisdiction and powers to the central Board, the chancellor, and the community school boards is confused and ambiguous. This legal defect has affected the functioning of the system during the first years of its operation.

A true test of political decentralization of the school system would require a complete rewriting of the legislation, giving community school boards control over the essential aspects of school policy. Many observers of the public school system in New York City claimed that the decentralization law served only to create an intermediary layer of government, which effectively insulates the educational bureaucracy from the demands of its clients. The virtual absence of real powers to the school boards in the areas of budget, curriculum, and personnel lends credence to this belief.

The decentralization law failed to grant community school boards enough power over personnel matters. That includes powers to establish qualifications and appoint, assign, discipline, and dismiss staff— all the while maintaining state laws and regulations. Crucial to these powers is an implementation of the Mansfield decision so that the boards would have necessary flexibility in choosing supervisory staff. Consequently, the Board of Examiners no longer fulfills a useful purpose. Indeed, under a truly decentralized school system, there is question whether a central Board of Education would any longer be needed. The state could assume the minimal duties of a central Board.

The community boards are also bound on another flank by the union contract. Central negotiations disregards the different needs of the various community school districts. More important, the community boards are wholly left out of negotiations dealing with such matters as teacher programming, lunch periods, class sizes, preparation periods, nonteaching chores, files, excessing, and various other details of school organization that go to the heart of the educational process. Innovation and experimentation are stymied by contractual rigidities.

The present custodial agreement prevents community school boards from having any control over the maintenance and conditions in their school buildings, or the costs involved, or the qualities or qualifications of custodians.

It is possible to have a kind of bilateral arrangement whereby certain contractual items, such as wages, can be uniformly contracted for by all the community school districts, and other terms and conditions of employment can be negotiated on a district-by-district basis. Until teachers' and other employees' contracts are made consistent with the needs of each individual district, there can be no successful decentralization and no community school board can be held accountable for the performance of the staff in its schools.

Under the decentralization law, CSB's cannot hire or fire pedagogical personnel at will. As for hiring, the boards must choose teachers from the eligibility list of the Board of Examiners, except under circumstances difficult to satisfy. In firing, prior contractual agreements between the central Board and the unions bind the boards' hands. The result is that teachers continue to be unaccountable to the local boards.

The CSB's, for the most part, have found it extremely difficult to wind their way through this maze. In spite of the constraints of the law, however, some CSB's have managed to attain and exercise a minimum of control in all three policy areas. For instance, some CSB's recognize that a principal occupies a key position in the administrative structure of the educational system. A principal is the liaison between the school, as a social process and community institution, and the community and between its professional staff and the bureaucrats above him. Most importantly, he sets the tone in the school. It is from him that teachers take their cue as to how they will relate to the children in the school. If his evaluation criteria of teachers are lax or his supervision of them is infrequent, the teachers' attitude to their wards will be similar. One wonders whether behind every incompetent teacher there is an incompetent principal. Thus by gaining and exercising control over the selection of principals several districts have overcome the obstacles in their path. As a result of the Mansfield decision, several hundred new principals are being appointed in 1972-73, and not from the central lists. Also, many assistant principals are being appointed. The possibilities to change in the years following are strong.

Similarly, in budget matters, the community boards have been invested with too little power. The central Board acts as a middle – man between the city and state governments and the community boards in budget matters. This arrangement has created confusion and rigidity and constitutes an instrument by which the central Board retains control over policy. Certainly, the community school boards should be allowed to have the power to let contracts for school construction, within the budgetary allocation, and determine construction and design details.

Budget is one area where the boards have been made particularly powerless. The formula for the allocation of funds to the districts, based on the average daily attendance, penalizes the school boards in minority districts the most. They receive less monies per capita compared to white middle-class districts, because their average daily pupil attendance is smaller. Consequently, with a smaller per-pupil allocation but with escalating problems of underachievement, the delivery of public education in these areas has a diminishing impact.

Although the decentralization law empowered the CSB's to take control of curriculum, its qualification subjecting the "choice of textbooks and other materials to the approval of the Chancellor," renders the grant of power empty. For there is a difference between curriculum improvement and curriculum change. In an article, Isaiah Robinson was quite aware of this, and to this end she took pains to distinguish between curriculum improvement and curriculum change. The former is concerned with

> discrete aspects of the curriculum without fundamental
> changes in its conceptual design or organization, whereas
> to change a curriculum means, in a way, to change an
> institution and changing an institution can be an unre-
> mitting, unrewarding task resulting in an inverse rela-
> tionship between input (plans) and output (products).[1]

One might have expected that school decentralization would contribute to the development of schools that would have become focal points for the community. It did not, however, result in opening the schools to the use of more community groups than under the old system or reduce the alienation of students.

The community school "serves the community as a center for a variety of educational, cultural, recreational and local social-development activity, for youngsters and adults."[2] The rationale for the community school is two-fold. First, the concept "reflected growing concerns not only about educational disadvantage, but also about delinquency, poverty, and general urban decay."[3] These problems are interconnected; the Bundy Report, for example, points out that "the well-being of children is affected by health services, and the physical planning of housing and local institutions is of concern to their parents."[4]

A second rationale for the community school is economic; it aims at making a more efficient use of school plant and facilities. Accordingly, "it is supposed to remain open day and night and to provide a center to which adults can come for advice and training, in areas ranging from literacy to skills development."[5]

The reason for expecting school decentralization to contribute
to the development of community schools relates to the experience of
the demonstration districts. These "districts sought more informal
contact with the community. In Ocean Hill-Brownsville, schools
maintained family rooms for the express use of parents. In IS 201,
the district operated their schools as a community cultural center,
becoming the focus of leading events in Harlem. Individual schools
often ran open house to familiarize parents with school happenings."[6]

Before school decentralization, schools were used for evening
adult education, recreation, and community centers. These programs
have been carried over, but they have not been significantly expanded.
Schools have been used as community schools in only a limited sense.
The school decentralization experience has not been comparable to that
of the demonstration districts.

Three reasons suggest themselves for the discrepancy between
the hope and practice of school decentralization. First, the CSB's
have generally not actively sought to open up the schools to the degree
necessitated by the concept of the community school. As we shall
see, they have been hampered in this regard by certain policies of
the city Board, so this charge warrants careful elaboration. The
present point is that the orientation of the boards to the community
school concept has not been activist or positive philosophically and that
this cannot avoid having practical implications. Consider the section
of CSB 2's by-laws dealing with the use of school buildings:

> The Board recognizes its responsibility to grant the use
> of school buildings and facilities during after school hours
> in the district in a reasonable and non-discriminatory
> manner equally applicable to all and administered with
> equality to all.

Although allowances must be made for the evasive, euphemistic, and
unexciting nature of the legalistic terminology that so often encumbers
the by-laws of CSB's, the commitment to the concept of the community
school manifested in this statement is certainly passive and lukewarm
if not negative.

A second factor that might explain the poor performance of
school decentralization vis-à-vis the demonstration districts in
developing community schools concerns the level of community participation in each. The demonstration districts encouraged and
realized parental involvement in the schools on a level never before
realized in our public schools. The experimental districts were what
many consider to be models of political decentralization. The present
school decentralization does not really compare with the demonstration
districts in the degree to which it has in fact opened the gates of

participation to previously excluded groups. This can be substantiated by noting the great impact of the Catholic church and the UFT on the school elections. Evidence that many boycotted these elections because they were being offered as an echo of the old system, not an alternative to it, is not hard to come by. Participation and power have not sufficiently been extended to excluded groups so that they might pressure authorities to move significantly in the direction of community schools.

A third explanation concerns the decentralization law more specifically. This law provides that the general responsibility for the care and control of school property will remain with the city Board. However, the "care, custody, and control of school property" is an ambiguous matter. Faced with budget cuts and rising costs, the city Board decided last summer that the law has given the CSB's power with respect to "the extended use of school buildings." This refers to the use of schools by Boy Scouts and other recognized youth groups. Whenever a school is used for such purposes, the city Board's agreement with the custodians' union mandates the assignment and payment of custodians to operate and maintain the plant. Although authority over these matters (the union contract) has not been given to the CSB's, they are yet responsible under the new interpretation for allocating funds for payment of such personnel. Because of this situation, the CSB's have had to charge community groups for the use of schools.

Before the city Board initiated this policy, youth groups that depend heavily on the schools for meeting places either used the facilities free or paid a nominal $3 fee for the year. The city Board refused to release the actual costs of these activities to the CSB's. This refusal, conjoined with the fact of general budget cuts, led many CSB members to suspect that the funds allocated for the extended use of school buildings would be grossly inadequate.

The upshot is that the city Board in this case decentralized the problems. It used the CSB's as a buffer to protect it from the outbursts of community groups who want to use the schools but would perhaps have to pay an excessive and prohibitive cost to do so.

What effects has the new policy actually had on these community groups? Several schools have barred such after-school activity, and some have had to raise fees. Disgruntled Boy Scout officials indicated that their group's growth had been "wiped out" because of it.

Nonetheless, some boards have cut down on the amounts they are charging youth groups, while charging full fees for adult groups that use the schools. Because the custodial union contract mandates a considerable charge just for opening the schools, many CSB's have encouraged youth groups to schedule their meetings when the school has already been opened by the CSB or another outside organization.

The matter of the extended use of buildings is perhaps not very significant in itself, but it does point to an area of friction between

certain community groups and the CSB' s that has the potential to
develop into a more significant cleavage. This, of course, hinges on
the adequacy of the funds allocated the CSB' s for this purpose. If the
charge for the use of the school plant is prohibitive, the schools can
hardly develop into "community schools."

The interpretation of the decentralization law by the city Board
has indeed limited this development. The CSB' s have sought to soften
the effect; however, this has been generally confined to support of
"recognized youth groups." If the schools are to develop into "community schools," the efforts of CSB' s will have to extend considerably
beyond this.

One important measure of the inadequacy of the decentralized
school districts has been the increased level of agitation among
parental groups for more policy input. The United Parents' Association, for example, changed its policy in this regard by strongly
recommending amendments to the law, so that only parents can vote
in the new elections (a crucial part of the Bundy plan). The UPA had
pursued in the past a moderate support of the concept of school
decentralization. At present, due to a grass-roots rebellion in its
ranks, it has gone as far as publicly demanding that union involvement
through negotiated contracts be halted, since this is an infringement
on parental rights to determine school policy.

Parents should be involved entirely in electing school board
members, and the unwarranted power and influence of the Catholic
church, the unions, and the political clubhouses should be eliminated.
The opinions of parents should be solicited and have more impact on
educational programs and individual school needs. There is every
evidence that public school parents still seek to expand their influence.
Certainly, the question of excluding the high school from the decentralized system as now exists cannot long continue without scrutiny,
for parents should be allowed continuity in formulating school policy.

In sum, our evaluation of the decentralized school districts,
since their inception, strongly indicates the need for a complete overhaul of the structure. Too little formal and informal power has gone
to the parents, and too little power has been granted to the community
school boards. It is therefore necessary that only parents, the true
clients of the school system, vote for community board members.
Further, the community boards should be given sufficient power.
Then, and only then, can one truly consider school decentralization a
reality and judge its promise, to better our schools, against its
accomplishments.

INTRODUCTION

1. Robert S. Weiss and Martin Rein, "The Evaluation of Broad-Aim Programs: A Cautionary Case and a Moral," Annals of the American Academy of Political and Social Science, CCCLXXXV (September 1969), 133-41.

2. Alice Rivlin, Systematic Thinking for Social Action (Washington, D.C.: The Brookings Institution, 1971), p. 127.

CHAPTER 1

1. Guiseppe Di Palma, Apathy and Participation (New York: The Free Press, 1970).

2. Marilyn Gittell et al., Local Control in Education (New York: Praeger Publishers, 1972), p. 2.

3. Leonard Buder, "U.S. Discloses Segregation Study Here," The New York Times, April 17, 1972, p. 13.

4. Bernard Bard in the New York Post, April 10, 1972, p. 17.

5. Ibid.

6. Ibid.

7. Bernard Bard in the New York Post, January 19, 1972, p. 9.

8. Ibid.

9. Leonard Buder, "School Unit Split on Examiner Bill," The New York Times, May 21, 1971, p. 24.

10. "School Board Turmoil," editorial in the New York Times, April 26, 1972.

11. Iver Petersen, "18 of 31 Dist. School Supt. Have Left Jobs Since Decentralization Began," The New York Times, May 21, 1972, p. 64.

12. Patricia Cayo Sexton, Spanish Harlem: Anatomy of Poverty (New York: Harper and Row, 1965), p. 13.

13. Francis F. Piven and Richard A. Cloward, Regulating the Poor: The Functions of Public Relief (New York: Random House, 1971), p. 274.

14. Sexton, Spanish Harlem, p. 10.

15. Marshall B. Clinard, Slums and Community Development: Experiments in Self-Help (New York: The Free Press, 1970), p. 327.

CHAPTER 2

1. Henry Levin, ed., Community Control of Schools (Washington, D.C.: The Brookings Institution, 1970), p. 289.

2. George Strayer and Louis Yavner, Administration of the Schools of New York City, vol. II (New York: The Mayor's Committee on Management Survey, October 1951), pp. 776-77.

3. Wallace Sayre and Herbert Kaufman, Governing New York City: Politics in the Metropolis (New York: W. W. Norton, 1960), p. 425.

4. Daniel E. Griffiths et al., Teacher Mobility in New York City: A Study of Recruitment, Selection, Appointment and Promotion of Teachers in the New York City Public Schools (New York: New York University School of Education, Center for Services and Off-Campus Courses, 1963).

5. Daniel E. Griffiths et al., A Report of Recommendations on the Recruitment, Selection, Appointment, and Promotion of Teachers in the New York City Public Schools (New York: New York University Center for Field Research and Social Services, 1966).

6. Marilyn Gittell et al., Local Control in Education (New York: Praeger Publishers, 1971).

7. Dale Mann, Administrator/Community/School Relationships in New York State, Final Report for the New York State Commission on the Quality, Cost, and Financing of Elementary and Secondary Education, August 1971, p. 34.

8. Arthur Vidich and Charles W. Reynolds, High School Principals Seminar, Final Report, U.S. Department of Health, Education and Welfare, Washington, D.C., February 1969, p. 5.

9. Griffiths, Teacher Mobility on New York City.

10. The New York Times, May 30, 1969, p. 25.

11. New York City Commission on Human Rights, Hearings [hereafter, Hearings], p. ii.

12. Chance et al, v. Board of Examiners et al, 70 Civ. 4141, CSD, New York, p. 3.

13. Ibid., p. 20.

14. Ibid., p. 22.

15. Ibid.

16. Reconnection for Learning: A Community School System for New York City, The Mayor's Advisory Panel of Decentralization of New York City Schools (New York: Praeger Publishers, 1969), p. 45.

17. Hearings, p. 21.

18. Progress Report, Board of Examiners (New York, 1962-63), pp. 2, 3.

19. David Rogers, Politics and Bureaucracy in the New York City School System (New York: Vintage Books, 1968), p. 495.

20. Hearings, p. 12.

21. Ibid., p. xxii.

22. Ibid., p. 17.

23. Rogers, Politics and Bureaucracy, p. 495.

24. New York City, Community School Board, District 15, minutes of regular monthly meeting.

25. New York City, Community School Board, District 4, agenda for August 11, 1971 meeting.

26. In Community Information Bulletin, July 1971, p. 1.

CHAPTER 3

1. A Summary of the 1969 School Decentralization Law for New York City [hereafter, Summary].

2. Marcia Marker Feld, A Basic Guide to the New York City School Budget Process (New York: Institute for Community Studies, 1969).

3. Summary.

4. New York City, Community School Board, District 24, A Report to the Community, No. 6, June 1971, p. 2.

5. Ibid.

6. Summary.

7. Strengthening Community District Management: A Pilot Study of District #14, Board of Education, City of New York, January, 1971, pp. 2-5.

8. New York City, Community School Board, District 22, minutes of June 1972 meeting.

9. Anthony Cresswell and Paul Irvin, "State Politics and Federal Aid to Education in New York State," unpublished paper, p. 20.

10. Ibid.

11. Letter to Helene Lloyd, Assistant Superintendent, New York City Board of Education, February 9, 1972.

CHAPTER 4

1. Leonard Buder, "Rate of Absences of Teachers Is Up" The New York Times, February 3, 1970.

2. Mildred Byrum et al., "Tracking and Homogeneous Grouping," unpublished manuscript, 1969.

3. Robert Rosenthal and Lenore Jacobson, Pygmalion in the Classroom (New York: Holt, Rinehart and Winston, 1968), p. 181.

4. A. Ballard, Balanced Class Report, unpublished, 1968, p. 187.

5. Marilyn Gittell and Alan Hevesi, The Politics of Urban Education (New York: Praeger Publishers, 1969), p. 264.

6. Henry Levin, ed., Community Control of Schools (Washington, D.C.: The Brookings Institution, 1970), p. 290.

7. Summary.

8. In The Advocate (Queens Lay Advocate Service) III, 2 (Spring 1971), 5.

9. Marilyn Gittell et al., Local Control in Education (New York: Praeger Publishers, 1972).

CHAPTER 5

1. Marilyn Gittell, Participants and Participation: A Study of School Policy for New York City (New York: Praeger Publishers, 1967), p. 7.

2. Ibid.

3. M. Fantini, M. Gittell, and R. Magat, Community Control and the Urban School (New York: Praeger Publishers, 1970), p. 78.

4. Ibid., p. 5.

5. Neal Gross, Who Runs Our Schools? (New York: John Wiley and Sons, Inc., 1958) p. 93.

6. Ibid.

7. Interview with CSB member, District 23, January, 1971.

8. Four Title I ESEA Evaluations: An Analysis of Management and Methodology (New York: Peat, Marwick, and Mitchell, 1969) p. 16.

9. Interview with CSB member, District 13, March 8, 1972.

10. Community School System Law Letter, I, 2, Spring 1972, 4.

11. New York City, Community School Board, District 7, Minutes and Memorandum of Resolutions, January 9, 1972.

12. CSB 7, News Release, October 15, 1971.

13. CSB 7, News Release, November 5, 1971.

14. Fox Butterfield, in The New York Times, December 25, 1970, pp. 1, 15.

15. New York City, Community School Board, District 10, Memorandum, May 7, 1971.

16. CSB 10, Minutes of Open Public Meeting, May 24, 1971.

17. Pierre Marique, Letter to District 10 Community Superintendent, May 24, 1971.

18. CSB 10, Minutes of Open Public Meeting, May 24, 1971.

19. Ibid.

20. Pierre Marique, Letter.

21. CSB 10, Newsletter, April 28, 1971.

22. Interview with CSB member, District 8.

23. New York State Legislature, Decentralization Law, S5690, A7175, 1969-70.

24. In the Amsterdam News, May 3, 1972, pp. 1, 12.

25. Ibid.

26. In the United Teacher, April 11, 1971, p. 2.

27. New York City, Community School Board, District 19, Memorandum: Procedures Used for the Selection of Acting Supervisors.

28. Ibid.

29. Ibid.

30. CSB 19, Minutes of Open Public Meeting, February 28, 1972.

31. Interview with Chairman of Community School Board, District 20, January 18, 1972.

32. Interview with Community School Board member District 21, January 19, 1972.

33. Ibid.

34. Interview with Community School Board member, District 25, November, 1972.

35. Interview with CSB member District 25, November 16, 1972.

36. Reconnection for Learning: A Community School System for New York City, Mayor's Advisory Panel on Decentralization of New York City Schools (New York: Praeger Publishers, 1969), p. 8.

37. Ibid.

CHAPTER 6

1. Robinson, p. 564.

2. M. Fantini, M. Gittell, and R. Magat, Community Control and the Urban School (New York: Praeger Publishers, 1970), p. 78.

3. Ibid.

4. Reconnection for Learning: A Community School System for New York City, Mayor's Advisory Panel on Decentralization of New York City Schools (New York: Praeger Publishers, 1969), p. 8.

5. Fantini, Gittell, and Magat, Community Control.

6. Marilyn Gittell et al., Local Control in Education (New York: Praeger Publishers, 1972), p. 10.

MARILYN GITTELL is Professor and Chairperson of the Department of Urban Studies at Queens College of the City University of New York. She is also Director of the Institute for Community Studies at the College. Dr. Gittell is co-author of Community Control and the Urban School and Local Control in Education. Author of Participants and Participation: A Study of School Policy in New York City; co-author of Six Urban School Districts: A Comparative Study of Institutional Response, editor of Educating an Urban Population; and co-editor of the Politics of Urban Education and Confrontation at Ocean Hill-Brownsville.

MAURICE R. BERUBE is a Staff Associate at the Institute and a lecturer in the Queens College Urban Studies Department. He is the co-editor of Confrontation at Ocean Hill-Brownsville and is a regular contributor to such magazines as Commonweal and Social Policy.

BOULTON H. DEMAS is a Research Assistant at the Institute and a Ph. D. candidate in political science at the City University of New York. He has published a study of the 1970 school board elections in New York City.

DANIEL FLAVIN is the Director of the Title IV Program in Adult Education for the Union Settlement in East Harlem. He has worked at the Institute and as a Maryknoll missioner in Peru, South America.

MARK ROSENTRAUB is a Ph.D. candidate in Urban Studies at the University of Southern California. He has worked at the Institute as a Research Assistant.

ADELE SPIER is a Staff Associate at the Institute for Community Studies and a lecturer in the Adult Continuing Education Program at Queens College.

DAVID TATGE is a Research Assistant at the Institute and a Ph. D. candidate in political science at the City University of New York.